P9-ARO-332

STUDYING SMART

REVISED EDITION

Time Management for College Students

DIANA SCHARF-HUNT
Ph.D.

with PAM HAIT

HarperPerennial
A Division of HarperCollins *Publishers*

FOR OUR HUSBANDS,
WHO ALWAYS MAKE TIME FOR US

"Time Slots" is a trademark of Timensions, Inc., and the phrase may be used only with the permission of Timensions, Inc.

STUDYING SMART *(Revised Edition)*. Copyright © 1985, 1990 by Diana Scharf-Hunt and Pam Hait. All rights reserved. Printed in the United States of America. No part of this book may be used or reproduced in any manner whatsoever without written permission except in the case of brief quotations embodied in critical articles and reviews. For information address HarperCollins, Publishers, 10 East 53rd Street, New York, N.Y. 10022.

First HarperPerennial edition published 1990

Designed by Ruth Bornschlegel

Library of Congress Cataloging-in-Publication Data

Scharf-Hunt, Diana.
Studying smart : time management for college students / Diana Scharf-Hunt and Pam Hait. — Rev. ed.
p. cm.
ISBN 0-06-463733-6 (pbk.)
1. College students—Time management. 2. Study, Method of. 3. College student orientation. 4. College students—Time management—Forms. I. Hait, Pam. II. Title.
LB2395.4.H86 1990
378.1'7—dc20 89-46505

90 91 92 93 94 TT/MPC 10 9 8 7 6 5 4 3 2 1

Contents

Part One

TIME MANAGEMENT FOR COLLEGE STUDENTS

1. What This Book Will and Won't Do for You 3
2. Time Management on Campus 5

Part Two

THE TIME SLOTS SYSTEM

3. The Four Forms Made Simple 23
4. Introducing the Course Requirement Planner (CRP) 26
5. Introducing the Project Assignment Planner (PAP) 38
6. Introducing the Weekly Time Slots 46
7. Introducing the Daily Time Slots 54

Part Three

TIMESAVERS

8. Study Time Tips 65
9. The Electronic Timesaver 74
10. Older Students, Other Problems 84
11. How to Get the Most Out of Even a Few Minutes 90
12. Other Ways to Use the Time Slots Forms 95
13. Visualizing Time 102

The Last Word 113

Part One

TIME MANAGEMENT FOR COLLEGE STUDENTS

What This Book Will and Won't Do for You 1

Congratulations! You've made the commitment to get organized! What you're holding is a guide designed especially for you, the college student, that will help you both to succeed in your studies and to get your life in order. We promise that this book will not waste your time. But we don't promise miracles. Like any new skill, learning to manage your time better demands dedication. The Time Slots®* system is an easy way to keep track of your life, but you must use it every day. Just as you won't see instant toning after one day of working out at the gym, you won't become instantly organized after simply reading this book. We encourage you to make this system a habit.

The Time Slots method includes four forms that will allow you to keep track of and manage your time. One is designed to help you handle your standard course requirements—reading, quizzes, exams, and so on; another is for planning special long-term projects like term papers. The third is to organize your week's activities, and the fourth to organize your day. Filling out four separate forms may sound like a lot of work, but it's not. If you stick with the system, you'll discover that spending a few minutes each day keeping track of your coming day and week actually frees up time for you. You will also learn how the forms can go to work for you outside of school, helping you organize extracurricular activities and fit them comfortably into your schedule.

We have tried to be concise. When possible, you will find "bullets" of information—quick tips to teach you the Time Slots system as well as to help you study more effectively, use a computer, plan a term paper, or manage your outside interests.

What will this book do for you?

---

* "Time Slots" is a trademark of Timensions, Inc., and the phrase may be used only with the permission of Timensions, Inc.

☐ Teach you how to get organized (there is a relationship between organization and academic achievement).

☐ Help you structure your studying so your homework is more palatable and meaningful.

☐ Enable you to face that early morning class prepared and without panic.

☐ Free your mind so you can concentrate on the task at hand.

☐ Allow you flexibility so you can enjoy unexpected opportunities.

☐ Help you feel positive about where you are heading.

☐ Give you confidence that you appear and are organized.

You will discover, as you use this system, how to make the 86,400 seconds in your day work for you. You will learn how to:

☐ Decide which are the most important tasks to accomplish, and then manage your time so you do!

☐ Eliminate many of the incompletions in your day so you aren't constantly trying to catch up.

☐ Take smaller bites in your life—dividing assignments or obligations into more attainable parts.

☐ Remain flexible even when you sense total chaos all around you.

☐ Eliminate overload.

☐ Use timesaving study tips.

☐ Cut through the confusion of new experiences.

There are some things that this book won't do for you: It won't be an A pill; take away your personality; wake you for a 7:40 A.M. class; allow you to cut classes; take the place of your brain; replace doing homework; guarantee an ideal roommate; cure acne or herpes, being overweight, or having romantic problems; make you obsessive, compulsive, or obnoxious; or neaten slobs.

It is, however, the next best thing to (choose 1):

☐ a hot fudge sundae
☐ sex
☐ a pushy mother
☐ natural brilliance

2 Time Management on Campus

College is a great place to change the way you think about and use your time. For one thing, you're on your own. There's no one to tell you what to do or when to do it. For another, if you don't get organized, you may not survive. Statistics indicate that, on the average, 10 percent of the freshman class—nationwide—will drop out. Counselors point to the inability to organize time efficiently as one of the most common reasons students fail to stay in school.

Actually, the term "time management" is paradoxical. In fact, time is a fixed quantity. It is always there, always the same. Time cannot be bought or sold. It must be spent; it can't be saved. Time can't be lost or found. The only variable you have is how you choose to spend those 86,400 seconds every day. Time management really means learning how to manage *yourself* with respect to time.

☐ TIME AND ATTITUDE

Few college students, faced with the reality of being on campus at last, think about how time affects everything they do. The amount of time a person has in which to do something—for either pleasure or work—often determines how he or she feels about that activity. For instance, if you head out the door for a 2-hour shopping trip before your afternoon class, you may feel excited and happy. Suppose, however, that you get caught in a traffic jam on the way to your favorite mall, sit in traffic for 45 minutes, and are left with just over an hour to shop. How positive is your attitude then? In the same way, time affects how you feel about your academic work. If you think you have seven days to read and study fifty pages, you probably feel comfortable about tackling the assigned chapters. However, if you discover you have just one day in which to do all the work, chances are you'll feel overwhelmed and anxious about it.

Many people find that it helps to see the relationship of time and attitude by imagining a balance scale with time on one side and attitude on the other. Generally, when you feel yourself running out of time—whether to complete an assignment or keep an appointment—you feel pressured, tense, tired, or even angry. However, if time is "on your side," you respond differently. You'll be relaxed, calm, "up," or even happy.

☐ TIMELY AND UNTIMELY HABITS

Much of the way we use our time is dictated by habit rather than by conscious decision. The conscious choices are easy to spot. If you have a class which meets three times a week and the professor announces that attendance is optional, you make the conscious choice to go to class and take notes because you want to get the most out of the course. However, most of our "choices" are actually habit; that is, we don't really think about how we are using time but simply act automatically. More than 80 percent of what we do is done because we have always done it that way. For example, although you may wish you could get motivated to do your laundry once a week, chances are you always wait until you've run out of socks before making that trip to the machines. You are acting out of habit rather than conscious choice.

Some of our most deeply entrenched habits involve the way we use time. How often have you heard someone say, "I always run ten minutes late," or "I know I'm a terrible procrastinator, but I just can't seem to change"? (Some people are habitual procrastinators. If they had their choice, they would put off having their own birthdays.) More often than not, even if we aren't always late or don't constantly procrastinate, we do not recognize counterproductive habits for what they are. It is by recognizing these habits and exchanging them for new ones that we put time on our side.

In high school Lisa got excellent grades by habitually pulling all-nighters before exams. A quick studier, she would cram to complete her course work and had always been able to pull As by adding a creative touch—writing an extra-credit poem or turning in an especially well-written essay. She started out using her old system in college but, within the first few months, discovered that the requirements were far more extensive. Another poem just didn't do it. Extra points meant more research and more reading. As her midterms neared, instead of catching up with just one particularly demanding course, Lisa was behind in all her courses. She realized, belatedly, that college was going to be four times as hard for her as high school because every one of her college courses involved either heavy reading assignments or hours of lab work. At this rate, she admitted, she would be lucky to pull all Cs.

This wasn't acceptable to Lisa so she reexamined her situation. She was able to identify two counterproductive habits which she made a conscious choice to change.

Lisa first had to admit that there was too much work in college to put it off. She couldn't depend on just pulling all-nighters anymore, a crutch which had allowed her to procrastinate. Then she realized that although she had been able to study in her room when she was in high school, studying in her dorm meant a constant series of interruptions. These two habits—procrastination and studying in her room—were working against her. The double threat of a 2.0 or 2.5 average and of her parent's reaction to that average was enough to spur Lisa on.

When she evaluated her study habits more closely, Lisa found that she was making good use of her free daytime hours. For instance, since she had no classes on Thursday mornings and her dorm was quiet at that time, she always used that morning to write and type papers and organize her lab work. But she ran into problems in the evenings. She always meant to sit down and study, but somehow her good academic intentions often turned into generalized rap sessions. She was lucky, many evenings, to get in one concentrated hour on her books.

Lisa made the conscious decision to make better use of her evening hours. First, she put herself on a nightly study schedule, concentrating on her assignments from 7 P.M. to 10:30 P.M. every week night, to change her tendency to procrastinate. She also physically removed herself from the distractions of the dorm by studying only in the library in the evening, away from the fun and confusion of her room. Thanks to her new habits Lisa no longer needed those all-nighters, and since she saved the dorm for socializing, she found she actually enjoyed her hours there more.

As you begin learning to use your time effectively, you too may need to change some of your old habits. This won't be an easy job. Changing familiar, comfortable habits takes commitment and a lot of hard work on your part. Admitting that it will be difficult is the first step towards effecting the change. Research shows that it takes seven to twenty-one days to establish a new habit.

Let's take another look at how Lisa did it.

First, she put herself on a study schedule, creating a new habit to replace the old one.

Next, she faced up to the fact that although she was used to studying at home, the atmosphere in her new collegiate "home"—her dorm—was fun but wasn't conducive to getting her work done. So she decided to study in the library.

Third, she announced her intentions to her friends and so felt duty-bound to carry through with them. (You are much more likely to be successful in changing your habits if you tell people you are doing so.)

And fourth, she followed through on her plan. While at first Lisa was enthusiastic about her new routine and able to carry it out easily, by the second week it began to wear thin, and when it rained three consecutive nights during that week, she was tempted to forget the whole thing. But she didn't, because she knew that if she made exceptions to the rule, she would not establish a new habit. By practicing her new study habit every evening, she reinforced it, and guaranteed its success. (Practicing a new habit builds consistency, which is why it pays not to cheat when trying to change your ways!)

By the end of the second week, Lisa knew her plan was working. She was keeping up with her work better, and she was happier studying out of her dorm. When she was forced to stay home because of a cold and felt disappointed at not being able to go to the library, she knew she had finally established her new study habits.

Soon even her friends noticed the change in Lisa. Instead of feeling pressured by her courses, as she became more comfortable with the work load, she discovered some academic interests and talents she never knew she had. Her new habits had become her allies, bringing out an intellectual side of her she had never developed.

To change your habits, remember the following:

1. You must have a new habit to replace an old one.

2. You must be vigorous in your follow-through, practicing the new habit every day.

3. If you tell the world what you're up to, you're more apt to effect the change.

4. As you see good results, it gets easier to persevere.

☐ ANTICIPATING THE DEMANDS ON YOUR TIME

Is it any wonder that college students can feel swamped? Between assignments and activities and part-time jobs and parties, who has any time to get organized? But you had better do so, since you are always going to be running against a clock—whether to meet deadlines or keep appointments or finish assignments so you can give yourself time off—and each of these demands on your time means added pressure on you.

One of the best ways you can lessen the pressure of college life is by realistically anticipating the demands on your time. If you know what you need to do and about how long it will take to do it, you'll be better able to plan and to implement those plans. Anticipating also helps you avoid *crisis,* which is the biggest enemy of any time management system. Nobody likes to get caught up in crisis management, those times when you go from problem to problem, constantly putting out fires. Everybody has those days occasionally, when you look back and realize that you haven't accomplished anything you set out to do, but nobody needs to have them often. While no time management system can crisis-proof your life completely, anticipating helps you avoid untimely surprises.

What kind of surprises? If you always knew what was going to happen and when to expect it, you wouldn't need this book. Time would be predictable. But of course, it's not. Still, if you are totally honest with yourself, you can anticipate some of the planned and unplanned time demands you may face any day.

Here are just a few situations which can—and do—happen.

☐ *Mechanical failures*—You're ready to head out to your tutor only to discover you have a bent wheel on your bike. You can't ride it. You missed the bus. And you can't make it across campus by 3:30 for that session. Or, as you put the finishing touches on that paper you worked on all night, the power fails and your computer crashes. You're back to zero.

☐ *Romantic crisis*—You open the mail to discover you've been dumped by your boyfriend or girlfriend from home. Your world ends and so does your plan to study for your astronomy exam.

☐ *Food emergency*—You are primed to study when you find you're out of soda and pretzels. How can you study without soda and pretzels?

☐ *Timing disaster*—You were positive it would take you an hour to read your literature assignment. It's been 2 hours and you're only half way through.

☐ *Work Strait*—You intended to leave work at 4:30 p.m., but your boss just made you an offer you can't refuse. Since a salesperson called in sick, you must stay until 9:00 p.m. There goes the time you saved to write up your genetics lab.

Any one of these problems can send your best laid plans into disorganization. The secret to effective time management is to be aware that glitches do happen. Smart planners are *flexible* enough to accomodate those unexpected and often untimely situations.

☐ THE BIG FOUR DEMANDS ON YOUR TIME

Let's look at some of those demands you will be facing this year so you can have an idea of what to expect. Generally these fall into four broad categories: *academic, economic, social,* and *personal.* Here's a sampling of each kind of demand. How many of them have you anticipated? How many do you know how to handle?

Academic

Since for many of you college is three to six times as much work as high school, you need to know some basic information so you can concentrate your time and efforts on your studies. Do you know . . .

1. How to choose courses?

2. How to choose professors?

3. The list of basic books you will need?

4. How to make your time in class count for you?

5. All about tests and how not to panic?

6. About grading and how to protest nicely without wasting your (or your professor's) time?

7. When and how to drop courses?

8. About cutting classes?

9. How to avoid overload?

10. How important it is to know your advisor?

11. Whether or not to form study groups?

12. How to assert yourself in order to get into a class, get help, etc.?

13. How to graduate with honors—special requirements besides grade point?

Economic

Money is always a big concern in college—especially when you are out of it. Make it a point to know how to handle each of these situations to avoid that financial clutch. Do you know . . .

1. How to open a bank account: saving, checking, credit, etc.?

2. How to budget your money? The object is to make your existing funds cover all spending categories for a specified period of time. If you have a lump sum for the semester, you lose if you call home for more money after just six weeks.

3. How much to allow for incidentals such as food, laundry, and telephone? It's not the big expenses that break your bank; it's the small, constant, daily costs.

4. How to look for a part-time job: where, what types to look for, how a job fits into your future resumé?

5. How to get financial aid and how to keep it?

6. All about scholarships: what's available, what scholarship searches can do for you?

7. How to start a business or service "agency" to earn extra money?

8. About tutoring and how much it costs?

Social

College life means that there is always something going on and somebody available to talk to. The social opportunities are mind-boggling. But if you anticipate these demands on your time you can enjoy the positive aspects of all this social life and avoid disasters. As you think about how you'll spend your time in college, know that you'll need to make time to . . .

1. Meet people.
2. Enjoy being with your roommates and friends.
3. Find the right roommate—if you have the choice.
4. Party!

You may also want to save time for:

5. Developing special talents.
6. Playing sports.
7. Participating in community activities.

Personal

When you lived at home, someone else probably made sure your clothes were clean, meals prepared, and so on. When you live away from home, if you don't pick up your shoes from the shoemaker, you won't see those shoes again. At the very least you'll need to know . . .

1. What services are offered by the student health facilities.
2. Where to shop for good food values and what brands to buy.
3. Where to shop for essentials.
4. Where the laundry facilities are and how to use them.
5. Where to rent appliances, furniture, fans, etc.
6. Where to get a haircut.
7. Where to find a good dry cleaner.

If you live at home, you may need to handle other demands:

1. What obligations do you have to family members?
2. What kinds of responsibilities do you have around the house?
3. What will you do about commuting arrangements?
4. Who will do your laundry?
5. What are your financial responsibilities?

This year you may be confronted by every one of these demands, which is why you need a method to help you manage your time. Let's take a look at the two most basic elements of time management, *planning* and *goalsetting,* and see how they can help you.

☐ PLANNING

Planning is the key to effective time management. To understand the role that planning plays in your life, take a moment to rerun the activities of an average day. As the images flick through your mind, ask yourself:

Do you start the day behind?

While you may have a good idea of what you want to accomplish, are you actually able to accomplish everything, or do you end most days with many "incompletes"?

Do you feel fragmented rather than all together at the end of the day?

Planning is the key to putting order into even the most fragmented life. Say you decide to try getting ahead one week by completing several reading assignments and starting a term paper in addition to attending classes. However, on Monday you get a call from the campus clothing store asking you to fill in that day, and since you can use the extra money, you do it. There goes half of Monday. Although you make it to class, you don't get any of your reading assignments done or your term paper started. When Tuesday dawns, you intend to complete at least two of those assignments and start the paper. You also need to run an errand, and you still must work your usual 2 hours that evening. But after your English lit class one of your friends asks if you can help him study for his anthropology test that's coming up on Friday. How can you refuse? Now it's Wednesday, and you wake up behind and panicked.

If you had followed a set plan of action, the scenario would have been quite different. You would have identified your priorities and understood that making that extra money or helping your friend might not have been as important as getting those reading assignments done and the term paper started. Chances are, you would not have ended Monday and Tuesday with so many "incompletes," or started Wednesday so far behind.

Of course, even with a plan you cannot always get everything accomplished that you want to. Planning will help you identify what really needs to be done. Since you are able to concentrate on those tasks instead of feeling pulled in so many different directions, you enjoy a sense of what you have accomplished at the end of a day.

Unfortunately, what most people think of as planning isn't. If they do think about what they want to accomplish in a day or a week, they rarely go beyond the "Must Do" list stage, jotting notes to themselves on a piece of paper. If this is your present planning style, it's a good first step, but this method doesn't go far enough. Making your list does not give you a way to get it all done. Nor does this method let you evaluate whether or not everything on your list even *needs* to be done that day.

To plan effectively you should first understand the two principles of planning:

1. Planning creates predictability.
2. Planning usually begins with long-range and moves to short-range goals.

Let's take a look at that first principle. Planning is the anticipation of what you need to accomplish and the setting of a course of action for accomplishing it all. Knowing what you are going to do and how you are going to do it eliminates surprises and builds predictability into your life. The Time Slots forms will be the basis of your planning. With them you will be able to see just what you need to do and when you will do it.

The second principle of planning means that you look first at what you want to accomplish over a given period of time—a day, a week, a month, or a semester—and then break that time into smaller increments.

Like Lisa, Tony hadn't thought much about time management in high school. But within the first six weeks of college, he knew he had to get organized. Tony's crisis surfaced Sunday evening when he checked his week's assignments and was reminded that he had a major genetics experiment to complete and hand in by Friday. Normally that wouldn't have bothered him, but this week he also had an English paper due and two junior-high soccer-coaching jobs lined up in addition to his regular class assignments. And he had promised Gregg, his roommate, that he would help him repair his car.

By applying the second principle of planning, Tony was able to make it through the week successfully. Here's how he did it. First he looked long-range and took note of the due dates of the two big assignments. Then he moved shorter-range, identifying which days he could devote to specific projects. He considered his overall academic responsibilities: He had classes Monday, Wednesday, and Friday mornings and afternoons, and Tuesday and Thursday mornings, leaving Tuesday and Thursday afternoons free. Since his genetics experiment was a priority that week, he decided to spend Tuesday afternoon in the lab, keeping Thursday afternoon free to complete any work and write up the experiment. He planned to write his English paper Wednesday night and cancelled a movie date for Thursday to give him ample time to type the final draft of the paper.

Looking at his schedule, Tony called the manager of the soccer team to say he could only coach the Saturday morning game this week. And he told Gregg he couldn't help him with his car until Saturday afternoon.

As you begin using the Time Slots method, you will see that the four forms build on each other, moving from long-range to short-range goals.

To begin planning your time, make yourself aware of the time you spend in class, studying, for your personal needs and social life, and even the time it takes you to get around campus.

Take a few minutes right now to think about how your day is divided.

- ☐ How many hours do you spend in classes?
- ☐ How many hours do you have for studying?
- ☐ How many hours do you have left for leisure?

You may be surprised, once you jot down the numbers, to see how your day adds up. (If the numbers add up to more than twenty-four, you're in trouble.)

☐ GOALSETTING

No time management system can give you time to do everything. Before you can realistically plan your days and weeks, you need to know what it is you want to, and can, accomplish. That's why you need to set goals to define what it is that you will do. Time experts know that having goals provides one of the clearest distinctions between those people who manage their time well and those who don't. A goal can be as simple and short-term as getting a term paper started this week or as complex and long-range as graduating with a 3.8 average.

Don't think, however, that unless you know right now what you plan to do with the rest of your life, you've failed. Long-range goals are important, but goals come in three handy sizes: immediate or survival goals; intermediate or future goals; and long-term or lifetime goals.

Let's take a look at these on a timeline.

Goal Timeline

Immediate (*survival*)	Present to six months from now
Intermediate (*future*)	One year from now
Long-term (*lifetime*)	Four years and on

For the most part, you should be concerned with immediate or intermediate goals. *Don't overload yourself with goals.* You are safest to concentrate on just one goal a week.

Setting goals and developing a course of action to meet them involves five steps.

The Five Steps of Goalsetting

1. State your present situation.
2. Write a measurable statement of your goal or objective.
3. Identify what you need to do to attain that goal. Think about all the activities, materials, resources, costs, or people involved, and consider any obstacles you must overcome.
4. List the activities necessary for you to carry out your plan of action and reach your goal in a professional, operational manner.
5. Decide at which points you are going to review your progress.

These five steps are the same for any type of goal. Let's walk through them with a couple of examples, first with an intermediate goal.

1. *State your present situation.* "I'm getting too many C's in my freshman courses."

2. *Write a measurable statement of your goal or objective.* "I will attain a 3.0 average by the end of my freshman year." When writing this measurable statement, make certain that it includes a date for completion and that it is:

- ☐ Reasonably attainable
- ☐ Sufficiently challenging
- ☐ Compatible with your values and priorities
- ☐ One you assume responsibility for
- ☐ Expressed as a positive action
- ☐ Stated in specific and measurable terms

3. *Identify what you need to do to attain the goal.* Ask yourself, "What am I doing now that I can change?" Your statement might read, "I need to organize all my course work by reading assignments, test dates, and research that I need to do. I need to find a study partner for Spanish and allow myself enough time to study for tests. I also need to talk to professors or TAs if I do not understand the material."

4. *List the activities necessary for you to carry out your plan of action and reach your goal in a professional, operational manner.* This takes you out of the amateur ranks and into the pro category. An amateur hopes that things will happen; a pro makes things happen.

Your list might read:

Get a study schedule together which tells me when to complete assignments.

Set up appointment with English prof.

Set dates to begin studying for tests on wall calendar and personal datebook.

Ask Sue to study Spanish with me twice a week.

5. *Decide at which points you are going to review your progress.* You may decide to set up checkpoints for progress in each of your courses after four weeks, the midterm, and three weeks before finals. At each evaluation, ask yourself, "Did this activity or project get me where I want to be? If not, why not? Did I plan the wrong action? Or come up with the wrong project? Was my failure a result of inadequate planning? Or did I set the wrong goals?"

At the end of four weeks you might find:

English—carrying a B+
History—C
Spanish—A
Philosophy—C+
Calculus—B

As you ask yourself those questions, you'll answer that your study project is getting you closer to your goal of a 3.0 at the end of your freshman year. The study partner in Spanish really helped. So has the conference with your English teaching assistant. But you will also see that you need to push harder in philosophy and history. Reviewing your study schedule, you may rearrange your time commitments to give more hours to those courses. If a C+ is the best you can do in philosophy, you may want to reevaluate your efforts in English to see if you can move that B+ to an A. Don't be afraid to adjust your plan of action at each checkpoint if necessary.

Now let's apply this technique to a more immediate goal. For example, one of your goals for a week might be to get into a class which is filled. You really want to take this particular class; you've heard good things about the professor, and this may be your only opportunity to study with him.

1. *State the present situation.* THE CLASS IS FILLED.
2. *Write a measurable statement of your goal or objective.* I need to be accepted into class so I can start it next week.
3. *Identify what you need to do to attain that goal.* Be assertive! Convince professor that I should be in this theater class because of my interest and experience. Get recommendations.
4. *List the activities necessary for you to carry out your plan of action and reach your goal in a professional, operational manner.* Call the drama professor for an appointment. Phone my high school drama teacher. Ask for letter of recommendation. Visit theater department to check on requirements. Ask English professor for letter of recommendation.
5. *Decide at which points you are going to review your progress.* Need to review by Friday—five days from now.

Using this system, you may appear at the drama professor's office the following Tuesday, armed with letters of recommendation to make your appeal. What if the professor listens to you sympathetically and tells you that the only space he has available is in an honors drama course? Remember the number one rule in setting goals: *Be flexible.* If you think you can handle the work, be willing to raise your sights. You'll be able to adjust to new circumstances. You can see how having a clearly stated goal and a plan of action saves you time and frustration.

Now that you understand why you need to plan and set goals in order to manage your time, you're ready for the Time Slots system.

Part Two

THE TIME SLOTS SYSTEM

The Four Forms Made Simple 3

Why *Four* Different Forms?

At first glance, filling out four different forms sounds like a lot of work. You will see, however, that each form has its own function quite apart from the others. What's more, each form builds on the others.

Some students complain that all this planning, setting goals, and filling out forms is "busy" work. It isn't. It's important. In spite of what you might be muttering under your breath, none of this is time-consuming. Scheduling should take you 10–20 minutes a day at most. The more you practice using the Time Slots skills and forms, the faster you'll become.

When Will I Do All This Planning?

Spend 15–20 minutes at the beginning of each semester to set up the course requirement planner. The project assignment planner will take more time: You'll need 20–45 minutes to fill out this form, depending upon the complexity of your project and the clarity of your thinking. Save 10 minutes on Sunday to fill out the weekly planner. And spend about 10 minutes each afternoon to fill out the next day's daily planner.

What If I Live at Home?

Live-at-home students have extra demands on their time. As you fill out the Time Slots forms, think about your own situation. For example, you will have to plan for travel time, both to and from campus. If you study at the library rather than at home, add travel time to your study hours. It's especially important not to over-schedule yourself. Since you juggle two environments, you are bound to encounter more conflicts for your time than a student living on campus. Consider those responsibilities at home. Are you expected to drive a family member? Do you do the yardwork, shopping, or housework? As you plan your time, always see what timesavers you can build into your schedule. For example, try to run errands in the same vicinity during one block of time. Then see if you can fit these in while travelling to or from school. When scheduling appointments and meetings, can you plan them during times when you are on campus for class to avoid extra trips? As you fill out your Time Slots, ask yourself if you are planning most conveniently for your needs.

Students who live on their own in a house or apartment have special demands on their time. Being independent sounds romantic. But it means more work, which means you have to plan for more time. If you don't have a meal plan or contract, you must figure in time to shop for food, cook, and clean up after yourself, clean your apartment, and pay your bills. Because landlord responsibilities vary greatly from city to city, you may also have to shovel the snow, rake leaves, and even make household repairs. Since all of these jobs take time, count them into your Time Slots planning. The more efficient you are running your personal life, the more time you'll have for academics and fun.

Time Tip

Always fill out your Time Slots forms in pencil.

Plans change. Good intentions melt away. Sometimes you may be more efficient than you expected; sometimes less. Using a pencil allows you to be flexible, and flexibility is the key ingredient for successful planning. Expect to change due dates or directions as you work on long-term projects. Expect that your weekly and daily plans may change. By using a pencil, you can easily erase the forms and adjust your time schedule. Copying over forms is a waste of time and energy.

Time Tip

Carry your daily Time Slots form with you.

If your Time Slots are always at hand, you can adjust assignments as needed. If you write changes on your Time Slots initially, you save time because you won't have to copy anything over later.

Finally, as you use the Daily and Weekly Time Slots forms, don't be afraid to leave some spaces blank. There's no prize for filling every line. The purpose of planning is not to fill up every second but to find more time for yourself. When you accomplish what you plan to do and have extra time, enjoy yourself! Don't automatically look for more to do.

Introducing the Course Requirement Planner (CRP) 4

Within the first few weeks of school, each instructor will give you a syllabus for his or her course. This syllabus is an overview of the requirements—reading, papers, exams, etc.—for completion of the course. The course requirement planner (CRP), one of which is used for each course, lets you assess these requirements and devise a systematic plan to meet them.

☐ WHAT THE COURSE REQUIREMENT PLANNER (CRP) CAN DO FOR YOU

The CRP helps you in two basic ways. It enables you to *divide to conquer* and *take small bites.*

With the CRP you think through each course, divide the requirements into smaller, manageable increments, and work on them in your own, most comfortable time frame. The CRP helps you plan, and it gives you a place and a method to record your plan of action. It lets you organize and visualize an entire semester or quarter of reading assignments, special reports, lab work, and presentations on a single sheet. Because you know what you need to do and when it must be done, it helps you fight procrastination.

☐ TIME SKILL NEEDED TO USE THIS FORM: ESTIMATING

Estimating how much time you will need for each assignment or activity is one of the essential steps of using the CRP. With all those assignments facing you, you need some way to figure out how much time each will take before you can decide when

COURSE REQUIREMENT PLANNER

COURSE: English Literature 101

Order to be Done	Course Requirement	Date Due	Total Time Est.	Date Start	Date Completed
1	Read Chps. 1-3 (Required Text)	9-18	3½ hrs	9-10	9-16
2	Outside Assignment - Library Readings	9-28	2 hrs.	9-16	9-20
3	Read Chps. 4-5	9-30	2 hrs.	9-20	9-25
4	Identification of Terms	10-2	1½ hrs.	9-26	9-30
6	Critique Chps. 4-5	10-14	2½ hrs.	10-8	10-13
7	Read Chps. 6-9	10-15	4 hrs.	10-9	10-11
9	Library - Outside Readings	10-17	3 hrs.	10-12	10-12
8	Midterm (Study)	10-20	10 hrs.	10-11	10-19
10	Read Chps. 10-12	10-24	3 hrs.	10-21	10-23
11	Oral Report (Prepare)	10-30	1 hr.	10-27	10-28
12	Read Chps. 13-15	11-5	3 hrs.	10-29	11-2
5	Term Paper	11-20	10 hrs.	9-30	11-15
13	Final (Study)	12-10	9½ hrs	11-20	12-8

to begin them. If you think about it for a moment, you will realize that you already do some casual mental estimating nearly every day. You may, for example, tell a friend you've got an hour's worth of studying left to do, or that you need to spend 2 hours in the language lab. We even measure distances in minutes instead of miles.

Determining how much time you need for routine activities is pretty easy. Count the hours you spend in class; you know you like to have an hour or more for dinner, that you've got a 2-hour lab on Tuesday afternoon, and that you work in the campus clothing store on Monday nights from 5:30 to 9 P.M.

Time *estimating* comes in when you have to factor in all the rest of your life—assignments, extracurricular activities, and other commitments.

Estimating Reading Time

Required reading alone—and most of your course work in college is reading—can throw a monkey wrench into the most organized person's plans unless you have some way of figuring out how to get it all done.

A simple formula for estimating how much time to allot for each assignment enables you to make educated guesses and to plan your time realistically. We offer here an easy formula for determining approximately how much time you will spend reading and underlining an assignment. (Don't worry if you over- or underestimate at first. As you practice using the formula, your skills will improve.)

Since it takes an average of 4 minutes to read and underline a page of text, this is the number we will use in our examples.

> Pages divided by days × 4 = Time per day

If you divide the total number of pages you must read by the number of days you have in which to read them, you will see how many pages you need to read every day. Multiply this number by 4 (minutes per page) and you will know how many minutes you will need to spend reading each day.

Let's say that you have sixty pages of reading in political science that's due in two days. Using our reading estimation formula, divide 60 (the number of pages) by 2 (the number of days) and get 30. So you will read thirty pages a day. Multiplying 30 × 4, you see that you've got 120 minutes—or 2 hours—of work to put in on that assignment on each of the next two days.

If you are a fast or average reader, use our suggested multiplier of 4 minutes per page to work out the formula. Fast readers might finish sooner, but they can always relax! If you are a slower reader, try doubling that number and allow 8 minutes per page to read and underline a text. Remember, the 4 minutes per page we use in the examples is an *average.*

For more accuracy, read and underline four pages of text, noting the time you begin and end. Divide the time it took you by 4 to get your average reading pace per page. Substitute your own reading rate for the number four in the formula.

Remember that subject matter affects your reading speed and comprehension. You may read a novel quickly, but spend three times as long getting through the same number of pages in a physics text. The one thing you can count on is that reading pace—even your own—varies.

Once you know what your reading rate is, you can also apply this formula to studying for a test or researching a term paper.

Using the Reading Estimation Formula to Prepare for a Test

Preparing for a test is a two-stage process: reading and then reviewing.

Reading. If the test covers 250 pages, you may decide to spend three weeks in preparation: two weeks covering the reading and one week reviewing those pages. Using your Time Slots skills, you'll divide 250 by 2 and know that you've got to cover 125 pages each week to get the reading done. Now decide how many nights you want to spend each week on the material. If you prefer to put in just two nights a week reading the text to prepare for this test, divide 125 by 2, and you know you'll have to read sixty-three pages each night.

Using the formula—*pages divided by days* × *4*—you estimate that you have 252 minutes (63 × 4) or 4.2 hours of reading to get done each week. You could spend 2 hours each in two evenings or, looking at the figures, you may decide to spend 1 hour, four times each week.

Reviewing. Continuing to apply this formula, you'll need to estimate review time for the third week. Reviewing should take you about half the time it took initially to read the material.

On the average, it takes 2 minutes to review a page of text, and this is the number we will use in our examples.

Allow 2 minutes per page for reviewing.

You'll move along faster during the review week. Since your initial reading time was 8.4 hours, you'll need half that time, or 4.2 hours, to review the 250 pages. Make sure to add some extra time to reread any of the chapters, go over class notes, and so on.

Estimating for Target Time

Not only does estimating give you a more realistic view of your work load, it gives you a target time for completion. Picture yourself in your room at home. Downstairs your family is watching the movie of the week. And you're stuck upstairs with your textbook. It's 7 P.M. and you've got fifty pages to review for that genetics test. Using the Time Slots formula and multiplying 50 × 4, you know that if you stick with it, you should make it through those fifty pages before 10:30 P.M. You sit down to study with a purpose—and an end in sight. While using the formula won't make genetics any easier (or make it any easier to miss the movie you've been waiting to see), it does help combat the I'll-never-be-able-to-get-all-this-done! feeling. And you will probably be able to concentrate better on the reading.

Of course, you'll have days when you won't make it through in the estimated time. Sometimes you may sail rapidly through the text; at other times, while waiting for an important phone call or recovering from the flu, you'll bog down. What do you do then? Just run the formula again, adjusting the number of pages to cover the material in the time that's left. Don't confuse estimating with total control. Don't waste time worrying over a missed schedule.

☐ SURVEYING: A USEFUL TIMESAVER

Like estimating, surveying is a real timesaver, and you ought to include time for this when completing your CRP. To make your reading time more productive, always survey whole texts and individual chapters. There is no formula for surveying, but after surveying a few texts and chapters you will be able to estimate survey time accurately by glancing at your watch when you start and finish and noting the number of pages you skimmed.

Surveying Texts

Surveying helps you understand how a book is organized. It also enables you to see the purpose of the book and the main thrust of the author's idea. Read the table of contents, the introduction, and the preface. Then skim both the first and last chapters. Check also for a glossary or index which will help you as you read the text. None of this should take you very much time, and whatever time you put in is time well spent.

Surveying Chapters

This helps you get an idea of the subject matter and how the chapter is organized. It also prompts you to have questions ready about the subject before you begin reading, which makes you an active reader. Whenever you participate actively in your studying, you'll get more out of it. To survey a chapter, read the title, introduction, summary, headings and subheadings. Glance at any visual material in the chapter as well. If the book belongs to you, circle words in italics or bold type. Find the main ideas by skimming the topic sentences in each paragraph.

☐ HOW TO USE THE COURSE REQUIREMENT PLANNER (CRP) IN SIX STEPS

Now that you know how to estimate how much time you need for your reading assignments, let's see how all this goes to work for you when you use your CRP. The following six steps summarize your approach.

1. Read through your syllabus and any other course requirement information. Note the major assignments and due dates for each. You may want to underline or highlight each of these in a bright color on the syllabus.

2. Write down these assignments under the *course requirement* column. Include the date that each assignment is due under the *date due* column.

3. Using the Time Slots estimating formulas, estimate the amount of time that you will need to spend to complete each requirement. When thinking about a term paper, you probably won't be able to calculate the time it will take you to research and write the paper in precise hours and minutes, but you should be able to mark off blocks of time (hours, half days or even whole weekend days) that you'll devote to this assignment. When considering research time, take into account initial library time, computer search time and interviews, as well as time to read and digest the source material once you've found it. Be sure to use the reading Time Slot formula to help estimate research time. Once you roughly calculate the time you think you'll need, write it down under the *total time est.* column. As you continue using the CRP, you'll polish your estimating techniques and be able to judge more accurately how much time you need.

4. Now take a moment to read over the columns and decide in what *order* you will complete all these requirements. A term paper due near the end of the semester, for instance, must be started well in advance. Be realistic when considering the time you will need to complete each requirement. Assign a number sequence to each requirement for that course under *order to be done.*

5. Give yourself deadlines to complete each requirement. Write the deadline under *date completed.* It's a good idea to make your deadline include some "fudge factor"—set it a couple of days earlier than you need to have it completed so that you aren't working down to the wire. By planning ahead and allowing yourself an extra day or two before deadline, you eliminate last-minute panic. As you work on the assignments, you may adjust the date completed date. That's fine—as long as your deadline doesn't come *after* the one required by the course syllabus.

6. Working backwards from your deadline, decide on the date to begin working on each requirement. Write this date

down under *date start.* Getting started is often the most difficult part. Once you decide to begin, start on that date.

Let's take a closer look at each of these steps, using an example.

Read through your syllabus and any other course requirement information. Note the major assignments and due dates for each. As you look over the English Lit 101 syllabus, you groan. The reading material starts with Caedmon's *Hymn* and *Beowulf* and progresses through Chaucer, More, and Spencer. Not only do you have required and outside reading to do, but you've got a term paper and an oral report as well. Reaching for a CRP, you write "English Literature 101" in the box marked *course.*

Write down these assignments under the course requirement column. Include the date that each assignment is due under the date due column. Reread the syllabus, underlining the major assignments with a colored pen and circling the due dates as they are listed. Chapters 1–3 are due on 9/18; the library reading, a short article on Old English, must be completed on 9/28. Chapters 4 and 5 are due 9/30 and you have written assignments due on both 10/2 and 10/14. Chapters 6–9 are due 10/15; the second library assignment—this one a ten-page report on a pre-Shakespearean poet—is scheduled for 10/17. The midterm is 10/20. Chapters 10–12 are due 10/24; an oral report on a poet of the period is scheduled for 10/30. Chapters 13–15 are due 11/5 and the term paper on an aspect of life in the Middle Ages in England must be completed by 11/20. The final exam, you note in red, is 12/10.

As you write the major assignments onto your CRP, noting when each is due, you see that this course won't give you any time to come up for air. You make a mental note that there's a quiz every Friday—you won't forget that. But you do write down when you'll have to go to the library to do outside reading as well as the dates that the oral report and term paper are due. You also include the dates of the midterm and the final exam even though they seem far off right now.

Using the Time Slots estimating formulas, estimate the amount of time that you will need to spend to complete each requirement. You'll need to survey the text, checking the table of contents and skimming both the first and last chapters. And you'll also want to survey the first reading assignment. You figure you'll spend 15 minutes going over the organization of the text, including the author's index and glossary of terms, and another 5 minutes surveying the first assignment.

As the average chapter runs about fifteen pages, your first assignment—three chapters covering Medieval England and Old and Middle English prosody, or forty-five pages—will take you about 3½ hours (45 pages × 4 minutes per page plus the survey time rounds off to 3½ hours). Then consider your first outside reading assignment, a five-page article. Being realistic, you figure it will take you 30 minutes to get to and back from the library and another 20 minutes to locate the article on Old English you need to read. You assume that you'll need a couple of readings to pull what you need from the essay. Instead of spending 20 minutes on the five pages, you estimate 40. Since you aren't sure of yourself yet, you round off the 90 minutes to 2 hours. Now, when you think about the second library assignment, a ten-page article on a pre-Shakespearean poet, you add an extra hour to your time estimate.

As you plan for each assignment, be realistic but don't worry about being exact. The CRP is a tool to help you plan; it isn't a rigid schedule. Besides, since it's filled out in pencil, it's easy to make adjustments.

Planning for the term paper. When you get to the term paper listed on the syllabus, you are tempted to put off planning for it. After all, the paper's not due for months. Don't skip this. The earlier you plan, the better the final project. Still, you are stumped. How do you figure how much time to save for a term paper? Estimating to the rescue.

Begin by analyzing the project. Most term papers are divided into three parts: Research, organizing, and writing. If the research involves four or fewer sources, you can divide the work load into thirds, spending one-third of the time researching, another third organizing and drafting the paper, and the final third writing, rewriting, and typing the paper. (If the paper required more than four sources, you would revise this estimate saving additional time for research.) This paper is short (six to eight pages) and requires only three sources. Researching these three sources should take about 3 hours of library research and reading. You add another 3 hours to organize and draft the paper and allot 3 hours more to polish and type it. As this is your first college paper, you throw in another hour for good measure as a fudge factor. You cannot imagine you'll have trouble coming up with a specific topic, but then again, you never know. Besides, interruptions are a normal part of life. Adding that fudge factor lets you anticipate interruptions and delays in your schedule. You round the time estimate off to 10 hours and record that figure on your CRP.

Now take a moment to read over the columns and decide in what* order *you will complete all these requirements. The order to be done column puts you into serious planning. As you reread the CRP it's obvious you must start with Chapters 1 through 3 in the text. You decide to follow this up with the library assignment on Old English since it is due next and is directly related to this reading. Besides, knowing you, if you don't get right on it, you'll be tempted to put it off. Then it's on to Chapters 4 and 5. By checking the date due column, you see which assignments need your attention next. You also know why you shouldn't panic. Sure, there's a lot of work, but if you take it in small bites, it should not be a problem.

Since the term paper is due in mid-November, and you hate to do papers, you give yourself extra time to do those 10 hours of work. Using your one-third approach, you figure on two weeks to decide on the topic (it takes you time to crank yourself up to write) and research it; two more to get it organized and drafted; and then you save two weeks to write and type it. Working backwards six weeks from mid-November, you decide you need to get this started by the end of September. You assign it fifth place in your order of business.

The only other special considerations you have are the midterm and final. You'll plan time for them as you get closer to their dates. But since the midterm will be over the first nine chapters you give it an "8" on your priority list, and you save studying for the final for the last.

Give yourself* deadlines *to complete each requirement. Beginning with number 1 and proceeding through to 13, set your own deadlines. These may be different from the due dates set by the course. Establishing your own due dates lets you schedule assignments on your own time frame. For example, as you read through your CRP you notice that the first outside library assignment is due on 9/28 and two days later, two more chapters are due. Here's where the CRP lets you take those "small bites." Since you have ten days between your first and second big assignments, you decide to give yourself a date completed of 9/16 for the first reading assignment, move the reading in Old English up to 9/20, and schedule the second text assignment for the 25th. As you work through the form, always check when each assignment is due and the amount of time each "bite" will take. Then choose the appropriate date by which you want to have each completed.

Working backwards from your deadline, decide on the date to begin working on each requirement. Write this date down under **date start.** Last, taking into consideration the amount of time you'll need to spend on each assignment, decide when to start each one. The start date acts as your signal to get moving. You will refer to it when filling out your weekly and daily Time Slots forms.

Keeping Your CRP Up-to-Date

Check your CRP weekly to keep it current. This helps you fine-tune your long-range planning. You can correct your estimates, plan your time more accurately, change deadlines, or add assignments you may have overlooked. Because you've filled the form out in pencil, you can easily make corrections.

For example, if the first library assignment only took you 1 hour to do instead of 2, note that on the form. If the second assignment, on a pre-Shakespearean poet, is comparable to the reading you did in Old English, adjust your next library assignment estimate.

□ THE CRP AND EXAMS

As you get close to exam time, you'll want to plan for your studying and reviewing. Here you apply your reading and reviewing estimating skills to come up with a rough idea of the time you need to devote to that course.

To plan your study time for the midterm, check your CRP. Add up the estimated hours spent covering the material up to the midterm, including your library time: Your total is 18½ hours. To review all this should take about half that time, or 9½ hours. You will also want to reread your lecture notes, so add another hour to go over those. You record the total figure—10½ hours—under *total time est.* for the midterm exam. Of course, if you feel a bit weak in any one area, you should add time for some extra studying.

To figure preparation time for the final, reach again for the CRP. Divide the course material into two segments. Reviewing the first half of the course—the Medieval period to More, which includes the midterm—should take you half the time it took to study for that first exam. Instead of spending 6½ hours, you'll need 3.25 hours. Now add up the total hours you've estimated to cover the second half of the course. This, too, totals 6 hours. But since you'll be reviewing for the final, and not reading and underlining, you cut that in half to 3 hours. Adding the two figures together, you estimate you'll need 6¼ hours to study for the final.

Since you are in the habit of condensing your lecture notes, add another 2 hours to review class notes, and allow yourself 8 hours to study for the final.

Comparing and Contrasting Your CRPs

After you've filled out a CRP for each course, compare them. Check for conflicts and overload. If you have term papers due in English and anthropology at about the same time, adjust your own deadlines. Plan to do one of them early in the course. Comparing your CRPs also helps you see how much time you have for extra activities. If you have two term papers and an oral report all due in late November, you may decide you can only do a smaller job for the Homecoming Committee.

Remember, this form is your long-range action plan. It can help you set your course and accomplish your goals. The more you use the CRP Time Slots, the more you will get out of it.

Introducing the Project Assignment Planner (PAP)

5

The project assignment planner (PAP) is designed to help keep those long-term projects—the ones that take at least a week to complete—under control. The PAP allows you to determine how much time you need for your project and helps you complete the CRP in a realistic fashion. You will use these two forms in conjunction with each other.

☐ WHAT THE PROJECT ASSIGNMENT PLANNER (PAP) CAN DO FOR YOU

What the CRP does for an entire course, the PAP does for a single project, breaking it down into its component parts to help you plan the work step by step. The secret of a successful long-term assignment is well-thought-out, advance planning. The PAP shows you how to organize your project and plan the time to get it done so you can do a good job and kiss last-minute panic good-bye. Like the CRP, it is a tool to help you fight procrastination. And it gives you a realistic picture of your time commitments for that project.

> **Time Tips**
>
> Planning creates predictability. Planning usually begins long-range and moves to short-range.

PROJECT ASSIGNMENT PLANNER

COURSE: Anthropology 101 (Prehistoric Man)
PROJECT DUE DATE: December 5
SEMESTER/QUARTER: Fall 85

Part	Project/Term Paper Outline	Analysis	Due Date
1	Library Research Topic	Reviewed 15 Books - Organize material - eliminate similar descriptions	11-5
7	Introduction	make bold statement about prehistoric man as basis for modern man	11-20
3	Definitions of Prehistoric Types	Listing of major types	11-10
4	Describing Prehistoric Man Types	Characteristics of Major Research	11-12
2	Meet with Professor	Says need broader topic / do "types of" i.e. a species	11-7
5	Similarities & Differences Prehistoric Types	Bring in how/where modern man has legacy of prehistoric	11-14
6	Conclusion	Ongoing research & its implications for our understanding	11-20
8	Type & Final Edit		12-1

☐ TIME SKILL NEEDED TO USE THIS FORM: ESTIMATION OF OUTLINING TIME

It is important that you become aware of how much time you need to do a quick outline of your project, outlining only the main topics; a fuller outline, including subordinate topics; and a detailed outline, with the ideas supporting your main and subordinate topics, so that you will be able to plan for those steps of the project.

> To outline a paper, plan to spend 5 minutes outlining the main topics, 10 minutes on subordinate topics, and 15 minutes on the ideas to support the subordinate and main topics.

Again, remember that estimating, by its nature, is an inexact science. As you work and become more conscious of the time you actually spend, you may substitute your own numbers for the 5, 10, and 15 minutes suggested to give times that are more accurate for you.

☐ HOW TO USE THE PROJECT ASSIGNMENT PLANNER (PAP) IN EIGHT STEPS

Now that you know how to estimate outlining time and how planning moves from long-range to short-range, let's see how all this goes to work for you when you use your PAP.

1. Each time you are assigned a term paper, research project, or any assignment that will take you at least seven days to complete, reach first for a PAP form. Write the name of the course and the semester or quarter in the appropriate spaces.
2. Fill in the due date and the project title in the appropriate spaces.
3. Do some mental calculations. Ask yourself these questions:

☐ What should the project accomplish?

☐ What kinds of research do I need to do?

☐ Do I need to talk to a professor or teaching assistant (TA) before beginning?

☐ Will this involve statistical data that might require computer time?

☐ Do I need to devise a questionnaire (and allow time to create it, distribute it, get answers back, and tally results)?

By asking yourself these key questions (and any more pertinent thoughts that come to your mind), you can see what's involved in the project.

4. Now break the project into smaller parts. Write down the major parts of the project as you envision them. This is a general, not a detailed, outline. List only the major pieces of the project and remember to *always write in pencil* on the Time Slots forms. The PAP is a planning tool. It's not a magic wand. Your research may take you in directions you could not foresee at the beginning. Don't be afraid to amend your plan of action as you get farther into the project.

5. Give yourself a deadline (due date) to complete each segment. Always allow a slight fudge factor to cover those moments when life gets out of control.

6. Decide the order in which you will begin each segment. Often this order follows logically as you plan the paper. But some sections, such as a glossary of terms or definitions, you may need to work on as your project progresses. In that case, you may want to start those parts of the project earlier, moving them out of their sequence to give yourself more time.

7. As you complete each part of the project, make brief notes in the analysis column about it. Your analysis should be a concise summation of your work up to that point—what you accomplished at the library, the major ideas you got from your reading, how you plan to relate your research to your paper, any problem areas, etc. These notes will help you keep on track during the duration of the project and alert you to problems you may be running into regarding subject matter, organization, or time needed to complete the project.

8. Once you have completed your research, reread your PAP. The "bones" of your project are now clearly exposed. You have done the major organizational work. Now, add the meat as you outline and write the term paper, prepare the presentation, or wrap up the lab report.

Let's see how this actually works.

Each time you are assigned a term paper, research project, or any assignment that will take you at least seven days to complete, reach first for a PAP form. Checking through your CRPs you see that you have a term paper due December 5. You write the course, Anthropology 101, by *Course*, and you write "Fall, 85" by *Semester/Quarter.*

Fill in the due date and the project title. Write December 5 by *Project Due Date.* You have decided that you'll write about a particular species of prehistoric man. You write that by *Project Title.*

Do some mental calculations. Ask yourself these questions: What should the project accomplish? What kinds of research do I need to do? Do I need to talk to a professor or TA before beginning? Is any statistical data involved requiring computer time? Do I need to devise a questionnaire? As you think about the paper, you know that it should show that you have a special grasp of some aspect of anthropology that relates to the material you are covering that semester. You would also like to impress the professor with your writing talents since you have not participated much in class. As for research, since you cannot go digging for artifacts, you are limited to library research. You feel confident doing papers but may want to talk to the professor or the TA about focusing the research. You cannot think of any other kinds of research or data you'll need.

Now break the project into smaller parts. You think through the steps you must take to write the paper on your species of prehistoric man and note them on the PAP. The first step is to go to the library and familiarize yourself with the literature on the subject. You decide you will want to talk to your professor about it before getting too deep into your research. After you note these steps on the PAP, you list the major parts of the project as you see them. You'll need an Introduction. You will define the type of prehistoric man you're writing about, and you will naturally write about the information you learned from your research. The paper must also have a conclusion. Finally, you must make time to type, edit, and retype your paper.

Give yourself a deadline (due date) to complete each assignment. Always allow a slight fudge factor. Remembering that planning begins long-range and moves to short-range, now target your own deadline for this paper: December 1. Next select the dates due for each part of the project. Looking at all that needs to be done, decide to give yourself about six weeks to complete this paper. You want to finish your library work by November 5, approximately a month before the paper is due. Working backwards from that date, you plan to begin researching the paper in late October. You give yourself a few extra researching days since you will need to check numerous sources. You plan on two more weeks to organize your notes and write a rough draft and save the final two weeks to type and edit the paper. Looking at these time segments, you arbitrarily pick 11/20 as the date to begin writing the first section of the paper.

Decide the order in which you will begin each segment. Often this order follows logically as you plan the paper. You begin by researching your paper at the library. That is step 1 on your PAP. You decide you'll talk to your professor early on, since this can save you time in the long run, helping you avoid going up blind alleys or choosing topics which are either too broad or too narrow in focus. You write step 2 next to meeting with your professor on the PAP.

As you consider the order in which you will write the paper and the most important ideas you will cover, you divide the paper into its major parts. You'll begin by defining a type of prehistoric man, describing him, and ultimately comparing and contrasting him to another type. These become steps 3, 4, and 5. Once the body of the paper is written, you will write the conclusion. This is step 6. Step 7 is writing the introduction. You find it's more efficient to tie the introduction to the paper than to try to write a paper around an introduction. Finally, you allow yourself time for retyping, editing, etc., and you pencil in Step 8 on the PAP for that effort.

As you complete each part of the project, make brief notes in the analysis column about it. In the very beginning of your work you run into your first problem. At the library you do a computer search. The abstracts indicate that your topic is too narrow. You note that the literature is too scarce and realize that instead of a particular type of prehistoric man, you should focus on *types* of prehistoric man. You adjust your PAP to show this new, broader topic, erasing the previous outline. Thinking through this expanded topic, you see the paper falling into place. You will still write an introduction, of course. You will then define the types of prehistoric men, identify certain main types, describe these types, and then compare and contrast them. You will also write a conclusion. You note each of these main segments on the PAP. As you research, you write a brief research analysis on the PAP. Under library research, you note that you reviewed fifteen books and articles, organized the material, eliminated similar descriptions, and focused on the most important writings. Not only does this analysis column help you see where you've been, this column shows you where you're heading. When you discover a fascinating article which links weather changes to evolution, you know that while you might enjoy reading it, the article is extraneous for this paper.

Reread your PAP. After completing the research, use your notes to develop the information on your PAP into a more formal outline which includes the main topic, subordinate topics, and ideas to support the main and subordinate topics. To plan time for this, use the Time Slots outlining estimate formula on page 40.

□ PROJECT TIMESAVERS

Here are some tips for saving time on written projects.

Writing Timesavers

□ Make sure you know the required length of the paper. This will help you determine the topic and define your perspective.

□ When writing, keep to the point of your paper. Check your PAP frequently. Ask yourself, "Does this really pertain to the subject I am writing about, and does it contribute to the purpose of the paper?"

□ Start with the first draft. Using your outline as a guide, just get your ideas down on paper. Don't get hung up too early on perfection.

□ Revise. Put that first draft aside for a day and then read it again to determine if you are on track. Make the necessary changes or as many revisions as possible for final draft.

Oral Presentation Timesavers

To prepare an oral report, many of the same timesaving techniques apply.

☐ Make sure you know how long the speech must be.

☐ Make certain your notes keep to the point. Ask yourself, "Does this really pertain to the subject I am speaking about, and does it contribute to the point of my presentation?"

☐ Research the subject as you would a written report.

☐ HOW THE CRP AND PAP WORK TOGETHER

The CRP outlines everything you need to do for a course, while the PAP takes care of papers, projects, or oral reports. In this way the PAP keeps traffic flowing for your CRP. By breaking a big project into manageable bites, the PAP, like the CRP, helps fight procrastination.

As you use these Time Slots forms together, you'll find that you can eliminate surprises in your course schedule—such as a paper that you meant to start but didn't.

Should you find that you have two papers or a term paper and report due for two different courses around the same time, the PAP enables **you** to decide when to start each project. You can easily move your deadlines around to avoid time crunches. If you can help it, don't attempt to work on two or more projects at once. Focus your train of thought on just one project at a time for best results.

Now that you have done your long-range planning, you are ready to move in to closer-range by organizing your weekly planner Time Slots.

Introducing the Weekly Time Slots 6

The weekly planner is your blueprint for the week. You will refer to it every day when you fill in your daily Time Slots.

☐ WHAT THE WEEKLY PLANNER CAN DO FOR YOU

The weekly planner enables you to effectively use your time to meet all your academic, economic, social, and personal responsibilities. Of course, you have to study, but you may need that part-time job and you still should have some fun. The weekly Time Slots helps you make smart choices about how you'll spend your time.

This Time Slots planner builds predictability into your life so you avoid those crunches—the I'll-never-get-everything-done days. By giving you an overview of your week, you can readily see which are your heavy days and which ones are less demanding. This form helps you minimize surprises and conveniently schedule interruptions in your studying for all those activities you enjoy. The predictability of weekly planning is reassuring. You know that you have plenty of time to meet your most important commitments and, instead of feeling pressured, you feel prepared.

☐ WHAT YOU NEED TO KNOW TO COMPLETE THIS FORM: *PRIME TIME—* ARE YOU A LARK OR AN OWL?

Our personal inner clocks run on different cycles. Some of us are larks—morning or daytime creatures; others are owls—those who come awake in the afternoon and evening. To plan your

DAILY PLANNER

PLAN FOR: Monday

Time Record or schedule	B	A	Events
6		A-1	Anthropology Quiz
7 Exercise/Run		A-2	Anthropology Class
8 Anthropology		A-3	Speech
9 Speech		A-6	Buy deodorant
10 Library		A-4	Art History Class
11		A-5	Library Study
12 Lunch / Buy deodorant	B-2		Call Home
1 Art History	B-1		Exercise/Run
2 Professor Smith		A-7	Meet w/Professor Smith
3	B-3		Post Office Stamps
4 Study Anthro Quiz	B-4		Start Anthropology Term Paper
5	B-5		Pick up tape from John
6 Call Home / Dinner			Bank
7 Study/			Cleaners
8 Library			Birthday Gift
9			
10			

time effectively, you must know which you are. If you don't, ask yourself:

☐ Do you get your best studying done in the morning hours?

☐ Do you come alive at night?

☐ When are you most alert? Which classes do you almost never doze in? What hours are these held? When you're at the library, what time of day or evening do you usually find most productive for you?

☐ When is your energy level highest? If you don't know, ask yourself when you would schedule an active sports event—an important tennis match, for instance—in the morning, afternoon, or evening?

As you answer these questions, you'll begin to understand your own inner clock and appreciate the fact that all days are not divided equally. This is important to bear in mind when you complete the weekly planner.

☐ HOW TO USE THE WEEKLY PLANNER IN FIVE STEPS

1. Set aside 10–15 minutes every Sunday to think about the coming week. Ask yourself which are the most important activities you need to do this week. Read over your CRP and PAP Time Slots to check for coming academic commitments—assignments that are due, papers to start, etc. You won't be writing these on the form in detail. Reading them over refreshes your memory to give you a realistic picture of the study hours needed for that week. (As you go through your CRPs and PAPs to plan your week, you may want to keep five daily Time Slots handy, one for each weekday in the coming week. As you spot specific due dates for starting or completing assignments, write these commitments on the appropriate daily Time Slots. This gives you a head start on your daily planning.)

2. Write in all your "fixed-time" hours first. Think of your academic and economic commitments. When do you have class? Any labs? What hours do you work at a job? Write these "fixed" activities under the appropriate day of the week and time of day—i.e., A.M. or P.M. on the Time Slots. Add any extra

blocks of study time and library research as indicated by your CRPs and PAPs. Again, generally think about whether you prefer to go to the library or lab in the morning, afternoon, or evening. Although it is not necessary to record exact times (e.g., English Lit., 8:40–9:30) on this Time Slots planner, if you find it helpful, do include specific hours.

3. Next write in all your "choice time" activities. Think about your social life and those nitty-gritty things you have to do for yourself. When do you do laundry, work out, jog? What extracurricular activities do you do? Is there a special movie that week you've been waiting to see? Do you need to run a number of errands? What about dates? List these under the appropriate day of the week and time of day you plan to do them. Don't be too specific, however. For instance, if you do errands Saturday morning, write "Errands" on the A.M. portion of the Time Slots. Don't list everything you plan to accomplish.

4. Block out large spaces of time for studying. As you do, think about the time you are at your best, your *prime time.* Remember to try to plan your most important projects and studying during your most productive hours.

If you fall asleep by 8 P.M., don't leave study blocks for 8:30 P.M. to midnight. Be honest. While it would be terrific if you were equally alert and energetic at all hours, you aren't. When filling out your weekly planner allow 2 hours studying time for each 1 hour spent in class. This is not a hard and fast rule but simply a suggestion. Some courses require much less outside work; others require more. But as you use the weekly planner to plan your blocks of study time, you're safer using the 2:1 ratio until you get the feel of a new course.

5. Now analyze your week. You can't change your "fixed-time" activities. But you may need to rearrange those choice hours.

First, look at the blocks of time you are saving for studying. Academics must be your number one priority. Are you giving these your best hours? Staring at pages with half-closed eyes is not the same as digesting the material. As you read over your weekly plan, be critical.

☐ Do your social activities interfere with your study times?
☐ Are you satisfied with the mix of work and fun?
☐ Are you overloading yourself on certain days?

Here's where that pencil is invaluable. If you need to juggle some commitments, erase the old and write in the new.

Be sure to use the flip side of the Weekly Planner for the following week.

Let's see how this actually works.

Set aside 10–15 minutes every Sunday to think about the coming week. On Sunday as you begin to plan your coming week, you review your CRPs and PAPs. Your CRPs indicate that this week you have English assignments, art history slides to identify, and reading in political science. Your PAPs show you that you have a speech to prepare and an Anthropology term paper to start.

Write in all your "fixed-time" hours first. You begin by filling in your class hours. Monday, Wednesday, and Friday morning you have Anthropology and Speech. Tuesday and Thursday mornings, Political Science and English. You have Art History Monday, Wednesday, and Friday afternoons. You congratulate yourself again on having gotten into all the classes you wanted! Since you don't have a job, that takes care of the fixed times.

Next write in all your "choice-time" activities. Here you consider the things you like to do regularly, all your fun or necessary activities. Without regular exercise your brain atrophies. You run weekend mornings and Thursday afternoons. You have a standing racquetball game Friday afternoon and this week, another game Saturday afternoon. You don't want to miss the basketball game Tuesday evening; there's a great foreign film at the Student Union Thursday night; and you plan to go to the dance Friday night. In addition you told your grandmother you would take her to brunch on Sunday. You also have plans for both Saturday and Sunday evenings. Your social schedule is packed. You write in "laundry" under Sunday A.M.

Block out large spaces of time for studying. As you schedule study times, you spot problems. You concentrate best in the afternoons and evening yet have plans for five out of seven nights. This doesn't leave many uninterrupted blocks of evening study time. You figure you can work on less demanding subjects during those 2 free hours on Monday and Thursday mornings, and use the time on Wednesday and Friday before lunch for errands and going over class notes, but you need those productive evening hours for your heavier subjects. You decide to use Thursday for library research this week and block out study time Monday, Tuesday, and Thursday afternoons. You also decide to work at the library Friday afternoon instead of playing racquetball.

Now analyze your week. Examine the time you are slotting for your academic life in relation to the hours you are using for your social and personal life. Are "choice-time" activities interfering with your "fixed-time" hours? Looking over your social plans, you have to say "yes." You do not have enough blocks of evening study sessions, so you forego the basketball game, reluctantly erasing that commitment from the form. And you decide that art history is more important than going out to dinner Thursday before the film. You plan to grab a quick bite at the Union and gain an extra hour for studying.

Giving the form one final glance, you make certain you've left yourself enough free time. Everybody needs time off.

☐ STUDY TIMESAVERS

Weekly planning assumes that after you've planned your time, you use it effectively. Yet, too often we daydream when we are supposed to be studying and worry about studying when we are supposed to be relaxing. To make the most of your study time, take a hard look at your powers of concentration.

Are you one of those single-minded individuals who plows ahead despite all odds? If you decide to spend that hour before dinner going over notes from your most difficult class, do you follow through or do you put down your notes to join your suitemates, who are into a heavy-duty discussion about who will win the upcoming game?

You can increase your powers of concentration. Here are some tips to help you do so and help you make the most effective use of your study time.

External Timesavers

☐ *Set up a study area you use for that purpose only.* This might be simply a corner of a room or a desktop. The important thing is that it is a place you sit to study—not to talk or sleep or eat.

☐ *Position your desk in the area of fewest distractions.* If your desk faces out toward the hall, consider turning it around even if you don't live in a coed dorm.

☐ *Avoid fatigue by using a comfortable, supportive chair.* Save on clothes, save on haircuts, but don't skimp on a good study chair.

☐ *If necessary, splurge on good lighting.* Just because your parents aren't there to warn you not to ruin your eyes doesn't mean you should ruin them. And it's difficult for your brain to wake up in the dark.

☐ *Keep the room at a comfortable temperature.* Avoid extremes. "Sweating it out" shouldn't be taken literally.

☐ *Break for exercise periodically.* A 2-mile hike every half hour is excessive, but a 2-minute stretch can do wonders for you.

☐ *Have all necessary supplies and equipment handy.* Keep your work tools at your fingertips so that you don't have to jump up in the middle of a problem to look for your calculator.

☐ *Work only on one class assignment at a time.* It's tempting to think you are SuperStudent, but splitting your attention only fractures your concentration. Put away your other assignments and concentrate on the one at hand.

☐ *Learn to study without background noise.* These are the days of constant background music, but research indicates that noise—and that includes music—does inhibit concentration.

☐ *Use the library instead of your room for studying.* Unless you have a room of your own or a roommate who is your clone, use the library for academics and your room for your social and personal life. You'll find that this way, you will get the most out of both locations.

☐ *When at the library, practice not looking up every time someone walks by.* Not so easy but worth learning how to do!

Internal Timesavers

Now that you're set physically, what about those inner habits? Make an effort to include these tips in your routine, and you'll be amazed at the effect they will have on your ability to concentrate.

☐ *Set a starting time.* Don't confuse rigidity with efficiency. Some days you won't stick to your schedule, but by giving yourself a time to "go," you'll find it easier to "get ready" and "get set."

☐ *Schedule all study time on your Time Slots forms.* Scheduling means you won't spend your day worrying about when you are going to get everything done. You'll know!

☐ *Set realistic goals for studying.* Don't overload or go too lightly. Again, as you learn to "take small bites," you'll discover what feels right for you.

☐ *Teach yourself to concentrate only on the task at hand.* Make an effort not to worry about problems with no immediate solutions.

☐ *Don't rationalize.* Eliminate common work dodges such as "I can't figure this out," "I was up late last night and am too tired to start this," "I can't go to the library in case that new person calls."

☐ *Avoid idle conversation.* Learn to be a Miser Mouth instead of a Motor Mouth.

☐ *Never use drugs or alcohol while studying.* Both dull your brain. A quick nap is better than a pill, and a 2-minute stretch is more relaxing than a drink.

Exam Timesavers

When your week includes preparing for an exam, find out the format of the test ahead of time. Ask if it will be multiple choice, essay, true/false, or some of each. Include time for the following on your weekly planner.

☐ Study by using *repetition*, which increases your memory retention. *Overlearn:* Once you think you have it, go over it again to make certain you keep it.

☐ Test yourself in writing. Make up questions. Take a 10- or 15-minute break from that subject, then answer them.

☐ Relax the night before the test. If you've planned your time well, you can!

☐ Review the test when it is returned to you. Schedule some time to find out where you went wrong so you don't repeat your errors. By making time to review your test, you save time studying for future tests because you won't have to spend time correcting past mistakes.

Now that you have your week in order, you are ready to take control of your days.

Introducing the Daily Time Slots

7

Your planning cycle is completed with the daily planner. As you move from long-range to short-range planning, this Time Slots form puts it all together for you. Where the CRPs and PAPs help you divide to conquer, and the weekly Time Slots builds predictability into your schedule, the daily Time Slots is your best protection against overload.

☐ WHAT THE DAILY PLANNER CAN DO FOR YOU

With this form you'll identify which are the most important things you need to do and decide how many you can accomplish each day. Like the CRP, the PAP, and the weekly Time Slots, the daily planner helps put your mind at ease. You'll be amazed to see how much better you feel once you get those loose "must do's" out of your head and onto paper. Putting your schedule on paper lets your subconscious "reminder center" relax.

> **Time Tip**
>
> Always plan the next day before it begins.

Planning each day before it begins has three practical advantages. By anticipating what you need to do tomorrow, you defuse potential crises: In general, you'll know what to expect. And since you've organized the next day, you can sleep more soundly. Finally, as an added bonus, you can sleep a little later the next morning since you won't have to get up early to do your planning.

DAILY PLANNER

PLAN FOR: Monday

Time Record or schedule		B	A	Events
6			A-1	Anthropology Quiz
7	Exercise/Run		A-2	Anthropology Class
8	Anthropology		A-3	Speech
9	Speech		A-6	Buy deodorant
10	Library		A-4	Art History Class
11			A-5	Library Study
12	Lunch Buy deodorant	B-2		Call Home
1	Art History	B-1		Exercise/Run
2	Professor Smith		A-7	Meet w/ Professor Smith
3		B-3		Post Office Stamps
4	Study Anthro Quiz	B-4		Start Anthropology Term Paper
5		B-5		Pick up tape from John
6	Call Home Dinner			Bank
7	Study/			Cleaners
8	Library			Birthday Gift
9				
10				

☐ TIME SKILLS NEEDED TO USE THIS FORM: SETTING PRIORITIES AND ESTIMATING

Setting Priorities

To plan your day you need to know which things you must accomplish that day and which things can wait to be done. In other words, you must learn how to put first things first—at last. This sounds obvious, but it isn't. While we usually mean to attack the most important tasks first and save the trivia for last, we don't. Instead, we do the enjoyable or easier things first, and by the time we get around to those things that really need to get done, time has run out.

Setting priorities helps you use your time more effectively by focusing your energy most productively.

The Time Slots system divides your commitments into two types only: all-important A items and less-critical Bs.

To set priorities, know that:

A = THOSE THINGS WHICH *MUST* BE DONE TODAY

B = THOSE THINGS WHICH MUST BE DONE WITHIN 5–7 DAYS

Estimating

Reading Estimating:

4 minutes/page = average reading time

pages divided by days × 4 = time/day

Reviewing Estimating:

2 minutes/page = average reviewing time

pages divided by day × 2 = reviewing time

☐ HOW TO USE THE DAILY PLANNER IN SEVEN STEPS

The daily planner is divided into four parts. The space on the right-hand side of the page, under *Events,* is your "to do" list. This is where you can jot down all the things you would like to accomplish that day, regardless of the order in which you will do them.

The "A" and "B" columns are where you'll differentiate between those things which must be done that day (your As—and those which can wait—your Bs). The left-hand column is your daily time frame or your schedule of what you plan to do when.

1. Take about 10 minutes every afternoon or evening to plan the next day's activities. Do not be put off by all these blank spaces. This is not a fill-in-the-blank test. You aren't expected to fill in every moment of every day.

2. Under the events column, *pencil in* all "fixed time" requirements: classes, library time, appointments with an advisor or a professor, etc. Refer to your weekly planner when writing this list. Don't worry about putting anything in order at this time. *The events column is a working list.* As you jot down your commitments, you may want to estimate the amount of time each demands.

3. Now list your other commitments for that day—personal appointments, dates, meetings, sports events, errands, etc.—on your working list under the events column. Here's the place to be specific about those errands.

4. Next, read over your events column list and set priorities. Decide whether each item is an A or a B. If an item is not either an A or a B, unless you have a really slow day ahead of you, don't worry about fitting it in. If you feel guilty easily, you want to erase those extra items.

5. Sequence the As. Number each in order of importance. As you decide which A you are going to do first, second, etc., write the number next to the A. Sequencing focuses these top priorities by showing you a plan of action. This step helps you avoid overload. Although anthropology is your first class of the morning, it's not A-1. Studying for the quiz is the most important thing you can do, and it becomes A-1.

6. Sequence the Bs in order of convenience. Remember, these are your second-level priorities. Be realistic about the number of Bs you can get done in that day. If you have a dozen As, you won't have time to fit in very many Bs. By setting your priorities—identifying the As and Bs—and deciding in what sequence to do each, you put order into your day. The more ordered your day, the less pressure you feel. You may discover, as you plan, that you have too many Bs on your schedule. Simply move some to another day. Remember: You have five to

seven days to get a B task done before it becomes either a Must-Do-Today A or obsolete.

7. Slot each commitment into the appropriate hour. You may want to run an errand in the morning or afternoon and not identify an exact time. That's fine.

Be flexible! Some days are bound to be hectic; others will flow more easily. If a day runs more smoothly than anticipated, you can add extra Bs to your schedule or just relax. Always make certain you have some time alone, just for you. You need time to climb off the collegiate whirl without feeling guilty. So leave some empty spaces on the Time Slots forms for a quick nap or solitary walk. As you learn to manage your time better, you'll work more effectively and discover extra time you never had before. Enjoy those free moments. You deserve them.

Don't congratulate yourself on your efficiency too fast. To make life run smoothly, you've got to put these plans into action. Carry your daily planner with you every day! Refer to it! Don't leave your action plan on your desk.

The 80–20 rule. To use your daily planner, it helps to become familiar with two other principles of time management:

1. Generally only about 20 percent of the activities on any "to do" list are top priorities.
2. This 20 percent usually generates 80 percent of your results.

Suppose you're out of class at 3 P.M. with 7 hours to spend. Dinner is at 6 P.M., so you have two blocks of time to deal with—from approximately 3–6 P.M. and 7:30–10 P.M. You can use this time any way you want to: run errands, shoot the breeze, study, go on a date, or do laundry—it's all up to you.

Your schedule for the day includes running a number of errands and completing two assignments which are both due the next day. Using the A and B system, you scan your list and decide that none of the errands rates as a top priority. You can pick up your shoes from the shoemaker any day that week, you've still got some notebooks, and as much as you would like a haircut this week, it really doesn't have to be done tomorrow.

Completing the two As, those assignments, will generate 80 percent of tomorrow's results.

Now for the Bs. If you don't make it to the shoemaker

before 5 P.M., remember you still have five to seven days to complete a B (assuming you have another pair of shoes to wear).

To understand how your daily planner works for you, let's walk through the seven steps.

Save about 10 minutes every afternoon or evening to plan the next day's activities. After supper, before you begin studying for the evening, sit down at your desk to plan the next day.

Under the events column, pencil in all fixed-time requirements. As you read over your weekly planner, you jot down your classes, appointments, any important assignments due, tests, etc. You write:

Anthropology
Speech
Art History
Meet with Professor Smith
Study for anthropology quiz!!!!
Outline anthropology paper
Study!!!

Next, list your other commitments for that day. You add these items to your events list:

Buy deodorant and toothpaste
Go to basketball game
Get birthday gift for roommate
Run
Pick up shirts from cleaners
Bank
Post office/stamps
Call Mom and Dad
Pick up tape from John

Read over your events column list and set priorities. Looking at that list, you can quickly pinpoint the As. You need to prepare for that quiz and go to your classes, and if you don't get some more deodorant, your social life will take a nose dive. You also must go to the library to study and meet with Professor Smith.

Since the anthropology paper isn't due for two more weeks, that's a B. You have a week until your roommate's birthday, and you do have other shirts to wear, so these are more Bs. You planned to run a mile every other day, and you did three miles the day before yesterday, so running is a B. The basketball game, you realize, may be off your list unless you get your studying done in time. You really should call home, and you should get to the bank by the end of the week—two more Bs. And you are almost out of stamps. If you have time, you'd like to pick up that tape and buy your roommate's birthday present, so you put question marks by those Bs.

Do you see how this system takes the pressure off? Instead of one huge list of things you *must do,* you have divided them into two, more manageable parts. Now you have only four As to do tomorrow in addition to attending class. And you've designated all the other items as lower priority, lower-pressure Bs.

Sequence the As. Here is where you order your priorities, reducing pressure and enabling you to accomplish more in a day.

Since your top priority in college is to meet your academic demands, being prepared for the anthropology quiz is the most important thing you can do that day. You write number 1 next to that A. You also must go to your anthropology, speech, and art history classes (numbers 2, 3, and 4), get in some library time (5), buy deodorant (6), and meet with your professor (7). You rank these in order of importance—As 2 through 7.

Sequence the Bs. Separating the As from the Bs isn't difficult. The hardest part comes when you are faced with all those Bs. Determining the order in which you are going to attack these helps you identify those *timekillers,* tempting Bs, and appealing "someday" things which are usually much more fun to do than the serious As. Sometimes as you identify the sequence of your activities, you may even discover that an item you thought was a B is, in fact, an A. Who wouldn't prefer to go to a movie than stay home and watch the dryer toss your clothes? But if you're wearing your last pair of Levis and socks and are down to the holey underwear, laundry—at least today—is an A.

Once you have identified the Bs, looking over the list you decide you must save time to run. You assign that B-1. You promised to call home and would like to get to the post office, start that term paper, and, if you have time, pick up the tape from John. You assign these items B-2 through B-5. Five Bs is enough, you decide. You'll wait to buy the birthday gift and to go to the bank and cleaners.

Slot each commitment into the appropriate hour. As you fill out your daily schedule, think about your prime time. If you know that you are best in the late afternoon, don't run errands then. Use that time to get that paper started. When you schedule those As during your peak performance hours, you'll be amazed at how much faster and more effectively you work.

> **Time Tip**
>
> Plan your As during your prime time whenever possible.

Be flexible! If you find yourself with extra time, add a B or two. Or just enjoy that free time.

Carry your daily planner with you. The best laid plans don't work if they stay on your desk.

Use your daily plan to avoid being distracted from the task at hand. Having your day planned allows you to concentrate on what you are doing. It minimizes that "I have to stop and do it now" feeling that can come over you when you are supposed to be working.

□ MASTER PLAN

At this point, you are so organized you can hardly stand yourself. However, there is one more tool which you may want to use: a large calendar which shows all the months at a glance. This will give you a place to record your Master Plan. The calendar lets you visualize the entire year at once—vacations, birthdays to remember, final exams, and other fixed dates which anchor your year. Write these dates on this calendar and hang it in a location where you can refer to it easily. If you share the calendar with roommates, each of you should plan to use a different colored pen to mark personal dates. Few rooms are large enough to hold two or more full-year calendars.

Part Three

TIMESAVERS

As you become more proficient at using the forms and managing your time, you will want to identify other ways to save time. To give you a head start, we've done some of the work for you. The remaining chapters highlight specific tips to save time when you:

☐ study
☐ use a computer
☐ find yourself with bits and pieces of time
☐ must manage more than just yourself and your college career

Last, we'll show you how the Time Slots forms can save time for you outside of class.

Study Time Tips 8

Your weekly and daily Time Slots confirm what you already suspect: Most of your time in college should be spent studying. Few people survive freshman year majoring in parties. By definition, making the most effective use of your time means your study habits must work for you. Good study habits can be one of your best timesavers in college. They can make the difference between high and low academic performance. Yet often we treat study techniques casually, assuming that somewhere between elementary and high school we have picked up the right habits and weeded out the wrong ones. Too often, however, this isn't the case.

☐ HIGH PERFORMANCE TIMESAVERS

Scheduling Time Tips

Schedule work demanding high concentration, such as reading and taking notes on a text, in 50-minute periods. Always include a break for conversation or exercise before resuming with a second 50-minute session.

Schedule 30-minute sessions for memorizing facts, figures, and dates. You may need to schedule several such blocks of time in your day to cover all the material.

Always allow ample time for library research. That way you can indulge yourself if you find more information than you expected and relax some if you finish early.

Schedule 50-minute sessions to get you through compiling notes and writing an outline for a short (three to six page) paper. Depending upon the complexity of the subject matter, you should be able to reread your notes and write an outline in this time. Add another 45 minutes or an hour to begin writing those first few pages while your creative juices are flowing.

Take study breaks. Include 5–10 minutes between subjects for conversations, stretching, munching out, etc. Let your brain know it's on a break and that you have switched topics before you buckle down for another study session.

Reading Time Tips

Read both for ideas and for details.

Make sure you understand how the text is organized. Once you understand how the author is approaching the subject matter, it will be easier for you to comprehend what he or she is saying.

Survey the text before you begin; and survey each chapter as you read.

Look for main ideas. You can expect to find one main idea per paragraph.

Note how the main ideas are organized.

Look for transitions which emphasize the main ideas, change the subject, and show relationships. Examples of these transitions are headings and subheadings, preoutlines which are used in a chapter outline, and enumeration, such as first, second, third, etc.

Watch for transition words like: such as, for example, to illustrate, to compare, in contrast, in addition to, etc.

Underline as you read if the book belongs to you. But use a pencil the first time through. After the chapter makes sense to you, use the highlighter to highlight important points.

Take notes as you read. Hand-eye coordination gets your brain going.

Use the OK4R method. This translates as:

Get an *Overview.*
Determine the *Key* ideas.
Read.
Recall.
Reflect.
Review.

Here is how the method works.

You have a reading assignment for class.

Skim it first to get an *Overview* of the assignment.

Determine the *Key* ideas from the subheadings in the chapter.

Now *Read* the assignment.

Recall the material by asking yourself questions about what you have read. One way to do this is to take the key ideas and turn them into questions.

Reflect by transferring the information you read into practical knowledge. Ask yourself, "Why is this important?" "How do these facts relate to the bigger picture" (i.e., the subject you are studying)?

Review by waiting 24 hours and then going through three of the steps again—Overview, Key ideas, and Recall.

Notetaking Time Tips

Take down as much as possible using your own brand of shorthand if necessary. Use abbreviations—e.g., à for at, = for equal, —, arrows, underlining, etc.

Summarize the major points covered at the end of each lecture.

Underline and asterisk to highlight important ideas and concepts. Do this in a different color from the one you took your notes with.

Try to get down at least 20 percent of what's said and don't concentrate on what you already know.

Get the facts down right. Copy data correctly.

Use tapes, but only run a tape recorder in class as a back-up system.

Keep one loose-leaf notebook for all your notes to be assured of having them when you need them.

Compress your notes, using your own words. Good things do come in smaller packages. If you space your study periods, you'll find that as you pick them up each time, you will be able to consolidate those notes into ever smaller, meatier portions.

Always put the proper date on the lecture notes.

Try using 3 × 5 or 4 × 6 index cards when taking notes for papers.

Listening Time Tips

Listening is one of our society's most underutilized social and academic skills. Why do we have so much trouble listening? Research gives us some insights here. It may help you to understand the problem by knowing that:

1. We listen in spurts. We tune in for 30–40 seconds, tune out briefly, and then return.

2. We hear what we expect to hear, which means that all our experiences and beliefs determine what we hear.

3. We do not listen well when we are doing other things.

4. We listen better when we are actively involved in the process.

Pay special attention during the first 5 and last 5 minutes of class. These are the most important. This is the time the lecturer usually gives a preview and the summary. If you pay extra attention at the beginning and the end, you'll walk away with a good overview of the subject matter.

Sit up front to be more attentive. It might not be as much fun, and you run the risk of having the lecturer know if you snooze in class, but sitting up front will pay off for you. You'll find that your listening ability improves with your proximity to the lecturer.

Concentrate on the lecturer. Sounds elementary, but it isn't. Once you make a conscious effort to try paying attention to the lecturer, you'll be amazed how often you slip and find yourself counting the perforations in the ceiling boards or following the cracks in the walls instead.

Tune out the speaker's mannerisms, voice quality, appearance, etc. Focus on what the speaker is saying, not on how he or she looks or is saying it.

Listen with your mind not your emotions. If the speaker uses a word or a phrase you don't like or makes a point which opposes your beliefs, don't turn the lecturer off.

Be prepared. Read assignments, study problems, etc., before coming into class so that you can spend your listening time concentrating on the issues at hand, not playing catch-up.

Think about the subject before you go to class so that you can anticipate what is going to be said.

Listen for ways to relate ideas to previous lectures, text, and personal experiences.

Seek answers to information you don't understand. If possible, ask the teacher after class.

Memory Time Tips

You are not learning if you cannot remember the facts and ideas you are accumulating. There are two ways to commit important information to memory—by rote and by association. Rote depends upon repetition and association involves your tying two ideas together in your mind in order to get them to stay put. To sharpen your memory skills, practice these *timesavers.*

Do not study when you are hungry, disorganized, or emotionally upset.

Memorize the right information. Be sure you have the right facts and ideas before you try to remember them.

Identify your alertness patterns. "Larks" study better in the morning before classes begin. "Owls" study better in the evening. Generally you have smaller alert-fatigue patterns during the day than you do during the night, which means that if you tire of studying, you'll recover faster during the day than in the late afternoon or evening.

Don't be afraid to sleep! Sleep helps you remember. Research indicates that a minimum of 4–6 hours of sleep is necessary for your best memory performance the next day.

Schedule shorter, periodic practice sessions rather than a single long one. You tend to retain things that you haven't finished memorizing, while you tend to forget things if convinced you won't need to remember them any more. If you have another session coming up, the material will remain in the back of your mind. Build your memory little by little. You'll remember more after five 1-hour sessions over five days than if you grind out one 6-hour cram session.

Plan your first review 5–10 minutes after a lecture, if possible. Do a second review later that same day. Schedule a third review one week later. Do a fourth one a month later and a fifth just before the exam.

Stimulate your other senses. When possible, use sight and sound. Visualize what you are hearing or reading, and talk about it with a classmate.

Be creative. Try to invent new ways to study material. Studying in different ways allows you to associate the material in a variety of ways.

Form or join a study group. This is only effective once you've learned the facts and ideas from your assignment yourself. Meeting and talking about your ideas with others enables you to get a more complete perspective of a topic. One good study group can be worth 5 hours of individual study.

Exam Time Tips

When taking an essay exam . . .

Read all the questions first.
Answer the easiest questions first.
Underline the important facts and key words in each question.

Always take 1 or 2 minutes to think and organize your thoughts before writing. Thinking time saves writing time and helps you avoid mistakes.

When taking a multiple choice or true/false test . . .

Answer the questions you are sure of first.

Don't spend a lot of time on any one question. Check the time every 10 minutes and leave 5 minutes at the end of the exam to go over your answers so you avoid careless errors!

Timekillers to Watch For

Often we don't realize how we sabotage ourselves. Do you ever indulge in any of the following timekillers?

Studying for a test while eating dinner. Chances are you'll remember the roast and forget the refraction formula.

Studying while straining to hear a football game down the hall. The score will be game 6—test 0.

Not understanding what you are studying but continuing to read, write, and/or calculate anyway.

Pulling an "all-nighter."

Studying while sleepy. Western Civilization won't wake you up.

Lab Skills

Labs generally fall into one of two categories: those tied directly to the material being studied and those which cover additional material which is not specifically presented in the text. Either kind of lab is time-consuming, and few students come to college with any real training in lab work. Now is the time to teach yourself how to put these timesavers to work for you.

Spend 20–30 minutes preparing for each lab session. You'll find that you can accomplish much more without panicking.

Before coming to the lab, note the primary point that the lab session is to illustrate or demonstrate. If the lab isn't directly tied to the material you are studying, survey the course quickly so that you can find how the lab fits into the course. Sometimes a lab assignment doesn't clearly define how you should begin. By understanding what the lab demonstrates and how this information fits into the course, you will be better able to identify the logical starting point for that assignment.

Outline the steps to be done in the lab. Look for time-consuming words like "prepare," "watch for," "let stand." These can throw your time plan out of sync if you don't plan ahead for them. Also, try to familiarize yourself with the vocabulary of the lab before you begin.

List the materials you will need for each session. Do you have to make them or will they be provided?

Reserve 10 percent of the time at the beginning and end of the lab for setup and cleanup. Use 80 percent of the time for doing the lab work.

Know at the outset if you need to save anything for the next lab.

Make a flowchart for each step in the procedure so you can record results in order.

Write down your observations at each step.

Get help as soon as you feel lost. Usually you don't have time to get "unlost" yourself.

Copy your results in an organized form as soon as possible after completing your lab.

☐ TWENTY TIPS FOR GETTING TOP GRADES

Sometimes students get so caught up in the details of studying, they forget the obvious. Here, thanks to Claude W. Olney, J.D.'s "Where There's A Will There's An A" seminar, are twenty suggestions to help you improve your college performance. You can obtain the complete program by writing to Olney "A" Seminar, P.O. Box 686, Scottsdale, Arizona 85252 (602) 949-9221.

1. *Go to class.* Do some fast math. Figure out how much each lab or lecture costs you—or your parents. The price, alone, should inspire you to get up for that 8:00 A.M. class. Need more incentive? Olney says that college graduates make over $600,000 more in their lifetime on the average than do high school graduates. Does that get you moving?

2. *Take subjects you enjoy.* Believe it or not, college should be fun—your classes as well as your social life. If you look carefully, you can find interesting required or "core" courses, even at the freshman level.

3. *Preview instructors.* Students who have been there before you know the good teachers. Ask and you shall find. Try to sit in on classes and check out instructors for yourself before signing up.

4. *Register on time.* Those who wait until the last minute may lose out on the classes they want.

5. *Buy the textbook before class begins.* Get a jump start by getting the text and reading the first fifty pages or so before the first class. You'll understand those first few weeks better and may discover you really like reading about the subject once the onus of "assigned" work is lifted.

6. *Pour it on the first two weeks.* Overstudy to get off to a great start. When you begin with As on quizzes or assignments, you get a taste of success. This builds confidence and keeps you pumping through the semester.

7. *Never miss a class.* Good attendance pays! Olney observed that, of his students, A students, on the average, missed less than one class per forty-five-class semester, while C students were out more than four classes in the same semester.

8. *Never miss extra credit work.* It's not "extra" if everyone can do it. Do extra credit routinely. This often means the difference between an A and a B.

9. *Practice taking tests to improve your performance.* Check out your school book store. You'll find lots of books on this subject. Take tests in magazines and anywhere else you find them. The more you practice, the better you'll do.

10. *Turn in your homework on time, neatly done and edited.* Make every page perfect. This tip also improves your typing skills.

11. *Practice memory strategies.* You just read some good ones a couples pages ago. Remember?

12. *If money is a problem, obtain student loans so you can study more and work at outside jobs less.*

13. *Present a self-addressed postcard to each professor after taking the final exam in each course with the course name noted and a blank space left for your grade.* Why? The postcard strategy has some definite psychological benefits. A professor is more likely to give an "interested" student an A if you're between an A and a B. And if your grade is close, this way you can discuss it with the professor before he or she turns it in to the registrar's office. Once grades reach the registrar's office, it's much tougher to persuade a professor to go through the trouble of changing a

grade. Does this system work? Yes! Olney says, "There are no ironclad rules on where a B ends and an A begins."

14. *Drop a course if it is not working out after the first week or so.* Familiarize yourself with your school policy on this, but don't be afraid what people will say if you drop a course. Dropping gives you the option to start that course again later when you are better prepared for it or add a different course right then. Don't get penalized with a poor grade for a poor class choice.

15. *Buy a pen with an eraser on it and use this for exams.* Your exam will be neater, and you won't feel as pressured to get it all down "right" as you write.

16. *Mark what you* don't *know instead of what you do know when you study chapters in your textbooks.*

17. *Stay fit and eliminate bad habits.* You'll get more out of your college experience if you feel good.

18. *Check with your professor during the semester concerning your grade.* Asking shows interest. If you are only getting a C, Olney suggests you switch to pass/fail. "If you are getting a D," he says, "get out fast."

19. *When taking exams, write as much as you know for an essay exam because volume does pay.* In a multiple choice test, "All of the Above" is a good guess.

20. *Don't take that lower-than-hoped-for grade at face value.* Fight for the close ones.

The Electronic Timesaver

9

A computer is a superb time-saving tool, and the more comfortable you become on the electronic campus, the more time you'll save. Today's machines are, in the computer vernacular, "user friendly." No, they won't guarantee you a date for Saturday night, but a computer can converse with you, if you make the effort to learn how to "talk" to it. Expect to sweat some during the learning process. And don't think you can learn everything at once. It takes time to become comfortable using a computer, but it is time well spent.

A recent report by the Research Institute of America notes that "in the years immediately ahead, computerization will spread more rapidly than electricity did at the beginning of the century." This report concludes that the challenge with computers is not to use them, but to figure out what it is you want them to do. If, as another writer observed, "computers are to the competitive business environment what the six-shooter was (in legend, at least) to the American Southwest: the great equalizer," whether you're a dedicated hacker (computer whiz) or electronically allergic, count on having a box and screen and some form of a keyboard in your future.

If you are already very familiar with your equipment, you will need to adjust your estimating, since you are able to do certain tasks (such as typing and editing) in 25 percent of the time you would need to perform that task without a computer. If you are not yet adept at using a computer, remember, when you are, to adjust your estimating accordingly.

Freshman who don't already own a computer should not rush into making that investment. You *can* survive that first year without owning a glitzy desktop publisher. But while you wait to make your decision, do some serious computer homework.

First, learn how to type. Until voice-activated computers are widely available, your fingers still do your "talking." Computer efficiency is only as good as your typing method, and even the slickest system breaks down if your hunt-and-peck method is too slow. Your best bet is to take a summer course in typing.

Generally, it's better to decide which software programs you want to use before deciding on hardware. Make it easy on yourself by asking your friends if you can use their computers to try out different kinds of programs. Borrow their manuals and skim them. It's amazing what you'll learn!

Before buying, try out different kinds of computers and software. Programs are idiosyncratic. Some word processors are easier to learn than others. Formatting options also vary widely. (Formatting means changing the way the type looks on the page, shrinking it or enlarging it as needed). If, for instance, you are planning to major in Japanese, check out the Japanese language programs to see which are compatible with the computer you are considering purchasing. Make certain you are comfortable using that program because, once you buy the hardware, your choice of software may be quite limited.

Meanwhile, invest in a typewriter with memory capabilities. This typewriter acts like training wheels to practice typing and precomputer skills. By your sophomore or junior year, making the change to a computer will be a breeze. And find out what your school offers in computer labs, printing facilities, etc.

One last tip. When you do make that purchase, make time to read the manuals both for the computer and the software. Don't wait until you are in a time crunch to figure out how to do something—or whether your computer can do that task. Most manuals are *not* written in easy-to-understand language, but it pays to struggle through them. Reading manuals thoroughly is usually time well spent.

□ THE COMPUTER—YOUR BIGGEST TIMESAVER

If you are computer-smart, you may want to put your project assignment planner (PAP) and course requirement planner (CRP) forms on-line. This way you can easily keep track of your progress, make necessary changes, and run off copies to post as reminders. Once you've set up these forms on your computer, you never have to worry about running out of Time Slots. The extra time you spend setting up the form on the computer is time well spent.

To set up the Time Slots CRP form set up a horizontal format of six columns: five narrow and one wider. For the PAP forms, set your page for four columns: two wide and two narrow.

As you format the CRP and PAP forms, store the blank formats so that you can recall these pages as you need them. Once the information is on-line, work directly on your screen to make changes and update information.

If you wish, you may also put your weekly Time Slots on-line. To do this you may find it easier to use a vertical rather than a horizontal format. Designate one narrow column for the day of the week. Set two wider columns to handle A.M. and P.M. Instead of reading your day vertically, i.e., with the A.M. section over the P.M. section, you'll see your day divided left to right. Once you format the weekly Time Slots, store your ruler settings so that you can retrieve this information easily.

Don't put your daily Time Slots on your computer. Yes, you can set up the schedule form and run off a copy every day. If you like to play on your computer, and you have the extra time, go right ahead. But this is a time waster. It's much easier and faster to use the printed Time Slots forms for your daily planning.

☐ COMPUTERIZED TIMESAVERS

Making the Most of Going On-Line

The computer has been hailed as the biggest timesaving tool since the eraser. And indeed in some respects it has replaced the pencil, typewriter, and eraser.

As you look at what you have to do, consider specific ways that a computer can save you time with words. A computer doesn't just print words, it "processes" them. In the process, you gain time and accuracy. Here are some of the ways using a computer saves you writing time.

Typing speed
Editing
Making copies
Checking spelling

Indexing
Outlining and Creating a Table of Contents
Footnotes and Endnotes
Professional appearance
Flexible formatting

Typing speed—It is mechanically easier, and therefore faster, to type on a computer than on a typewriter. With a computer you don't wait for anything to strike paper. As fast as you strike the key, that's as fast as the image appears on the screen. This may not sound like much, but at 11 P.M. when you have six more pages to type, you'll notice the difference. The typing process is also enhanced if you program keys for words and phrases you use frequently. Once these words and phrases are entered into the computer's memory, one key stroke brings them up forever, or at least until you take them out of the memory bank.

Editing—Computers allow you to jump anywhere in the document to change a word, sentence, or paragraph. You can even switch between documents, cutting and pasting entire sections with the push of a few keys. This ability to move paragraphs and change words quickly enables you to easily fine-tune your writing. Few students will consider using a typewriter to retype an entire page or two to correct a trite or repetitive word. But with a computer, you can make all those small but impressive changes easily. These kinds of changes improve your writing style—and your grades—dramatically.

Making copies—The first time you have to do a second paper on one subject, you'll want to kiss your computer. Having easy access to previous work is a plus for students who want to make the most efficient use of their time. You can pull up that old paper and "borrow" a few excellent paragraphs to incorporate into the new paper, rather than researching and writing everything again from scratch.

The first time a professor loses your paper (yes, this does happen!), you'll bless your computer investment. Being able to produce a second copy of that paper at a moment's notice is another boon. Because professors expect upper level students to use computers, they can be quite casual about a misplaced paper. Remember, in college *you* are responsible for yourself and all your work. There's no one around to bail you out. So being able to produce another copy in a hurry is not a luxury, it's almost expected.

Checking spelling—This feature alone is one of the best reasons for buying a computer. Make certain the software you are considering has a good spell checker. Most will also pick up double words, and some will also read for grammatical errors. If you are deciding on software, be selective about this feature since it is one you will depend on.

On-line thesaurus—Stuck for a word? Just a flip of a key or two and an entire thesaurus is at your disposal! This feature will dramatically improve both your writing and vocabulary skills. Make sure the system you are buying offers this feature and that you like the thesaurus that's provided—that its choice of words are the words you would want to use.

Indexing, which lets you list and sort—This is a more sophisticated use of a computer, but it's worth investigating. Whenever you must assemble a bibliography or a data base and need to put a list in sequence or sort in alphabetical order, you'll appreciate this feature. When selecting software, check out how easy or difficult it is to list and sort.

Outlining and Creating a Table of Contents—Computers can make these chores a breeze. Locate this feature and try it out to see how "user friendly" it is.

Footnotes and Endnotes—Never again panic about the proper format or if you have enough room at the bottom of a page for a footnote. Most word processing systems offer you both footnoting and endnoting capabilities. Work with the different software systems to determine your preference.

Professional appearance—Computers make "white out" largely a thing of the past. Moreover, papers prepared on a word processor produce a professional look most typists can't match. Since appearance counts in college, this is a practical, not just cosmetic, feature.

Flexible formatting lets you change your mind and your margins—both left and right and top and bottom—and even your typeface. Formatting is the 90's answer to writing well. It allows you to make the paper fit the assignment without being obvious. Thanks to the page preview (a feature common to all word processors), you can manipulate what you've written until you are satisfied that it fits the page as you want it to look. Smart, successful students spend time changing type fonts and page formatting to adjust the copy to the page count instead of writing fluff or cutting paragraphs.

In addition, you can save time by "talking" to other

computers for research and forming electronic study groups to exchange ideas.

When writing a paper, don't save your computer for your final draft. Make your writing changes right on the screen. Not only can you physically write faster, but since you always have "clean copy" in front of you (free of scratch-outs, arrows, notes crawling up the margin, etc.) you think better. A clean screen keeps your mind in order, and you'll find that as you use your computer, you organize your thoughts better and identify problem areas sooner.

Use your computer for repetitive tasks. Store paragraphs or statistical data that you use frequently in your computer library so that you are not constantly retyping this information. For instance, if you are involved in a fund-raising effort for a local political club, and plan a letter campaign stretching over a few months, you may store the "meat" of the letter on a disk so that you aren't continually retyping, "The Young Democrats is a club which . . ." etc.

Save and store any models you create for classes so that you can update or remodel them for later use. You may do a survey for an introductory marketing course one semester which can be expanded for an upper level course the following year. Or you may plan menus for a nutrition assignment which you can later take apart and put back together (thanks to sorting capabilities) for more advanced nutritional study. It's not cheating to use yourself and your own original work as a reference source!

Save your resumé on your computer. Even freshmen can put a resumé together. Then, once it's in your electronic memory, you can update it or change it as your experience grows. Having a resumé on computer allows you to reorganize it easily so you can emphasize different skills for different opportunities.

Create your own academic data base. Save all the written work you do in college on disk. You may want to color code those floppy disks either by subject or year or organize your hard disk that way. But do save all your reports, papers, essays, etc. You will be amazed how often you can reuse that information once you have it at your fingertips.

As soon as you can squeeze this in, take an orientation course at your school library to learn how to use your computerized research facilities. Investigate which research centers are on-line, and what each service offers. If such a course isn't offered, make friends with a librarian and find out about the facilities. Since most research services keep only abstracts online, inquire about the possibility of obtaining complete articles from an "off-line" service for information from publications which are not available in the school library. Computerized searches can be costly, so learn to do as much as you can for yourself to save money. Get to know your research librarian. He or she can save you lots of time and trouble. It's not cheating to have someone help you obtain information; that's what a research librarian does! However, if you have some knowledge of how computer searches are done, you can make his or her job easier.

If you haven't done computer searches, ask your librarian for individualized instruction until you develop a good degree of computer comfort. Remember, when doing computer searches, time really *is* money.

A word about printers. Although some professors may ask you to turn in papers on disk, most will want "hard copy"—that is, on paper. Access to a printer is essential. Many college students do buy a computer eventually, but not everyone can afford a printer. So check out the printer situation thoroughly before making your purchase.

Here are some suggestions.

If you plan to buy a printer, know that some professors refuse to accept work done on dot matrix printers because they have difficulty reading that type of print. Dot matrix printers are less expensive, but quality varies. At the other end of the spectrum, the best printer available today is a laser printer which produces a fine, clear "letter quality" image. The downside is that laser printers are very expensive. A good option is a "near letter quality" printer. There are many on the market today to choose from.

If you decide to purchase a printer, first check out the quality of the printing available in your price range. Are the letters easy to read? Are they uniform? What kinds of type styles are available?

Notice the speed of the printer. Is it very slow? Does it "type" quickly? You'll pay more for more speed, but very slow printers can be frustrating.

Finally, how does the printer look and sound? Is it very large? Is it noisy? If you are working in a small space, a loud clacking or high-pitched whine can bother you.

If purchasing a printer isn't an option for you, do inquire

before buying your computer what kind of printers are available at your school's computer lab. Then purchase a computer system that's compatible with the school printers.

Or, make friends with someone who has a printer that works with your computer. Offer to buy paper and ribbons for it in exchange for your using it.

Don't think, however, that a computer will solve every problem for you. There are many times when you would be smarter to reach for a pencil and paper. Once you are converted to computers, it's easy to get lulled into thinking that the entire world requires a disk drive to operate. Watch out for these computer time traps. While you may think you are saving all kinds of time and effort, you aren't.

As a general rule, don't use your computer to take notes while reading daily assignments. The manual hand-eye effort of writing the notes helps complete the learning connection. Typing notes actually short-circuits that connection and shortchanges you.

One exception to this rule is when you are working on a big project which requires many sources. Here a computer can be a timesaver because you can create typed notecards as you research. Some data bases set up notecards for you. You may also create your own. One student did this by noting the book number (from her own bibliography), page number, and subject at the top of the screen, and then typing long quotes and any notes she thought she might need as she read the material.

After completing her research, she changed the font size of the type and rearranged the information on the screen to fit notecards. She printed these pages, trimmed them to size, and stapled her notecards to index cards. Creating computer notecards as she researched saved time and helped her organize the paper more effectively.

When using your computer to do research, don't depend on abstracts only. Although it is tempting to skip those long hours in the library, use the abstracts as guides to steer you to the complete articles you need to read.

Don't think your computer is invincible. Always back up all material. If you have a hard disk, make a floppy copy. If you work on floppies, make a second floppy as back up. Hard disks crash; floppies can get lost or damaged. Don't be caught with only your original work.

Consider investing in a hard disk as soon as you can afford

it. Hard disks allow computers to run faster and operate more complex software. Take this feature into account when deciding whether or not to make that extra purchase.

If you do buy a hard disk, clean it out periodically by transferring material onto floppies and deleting this information from the hard disk. You'll prolong the life of the hard disk and will still be able to retrieve data when needed.

Train yourself to save information every 10 minutes or so. Many programs have an *auto-save* feature. Learn how to use this. The slight inconvenience of having to stop working for a few seconds while the computer saves the material for you is well worth the trouble. The first time you experience a problem and can retrieve your data from a saved backup file, you'll bless autosave.

Buy a power surge protector to keep your system free of common glitches. Electric current surges and wanes. Computers are sensitive to these changes. Sensitivity can mean big trouble for hard disks similar to what happens when a record gets scratched. "Scratched" areas on hard disks can create dead spaces which cause the computer not to work properly.

Don't use your computer to balance your checkbook unless you are a computer whiz and find this a snap. A pocket calculator, a pencil and paper, and a large box of tissues (for those awful moments of realization) can do the job just as effectively.

Above all, don't buy a computer until you know what *you* need. Individuals' needs vary. For instance, some students prefer laptops to bigger systems because they want to take their laptop computers into class to take notes on them. Other students may need sophisticated graphic capabilities to produce the necessary work in a major.

Be open minded. Computer technology is continually changing and improving. You'll miss out if you only consider one type of system. Browse through computer magazines; visit computer stores; stay abreast of improvements. Computers are one of the few luxuries in life that continues to decrease in price! Don't be afraid to change hardware or software. In the world of computers, you have no where to trade but up.

Finally, organize your computer carefully so you can retrieve material easily. Don't throw all your information and data into one giant "MISC" file. That's equivalent to opening a draw and tossing everything into it! You'll have trouble finding information when you want it. Computers are *not* magic. You can lose things as easily in a computer as you can in a sloppy desk!

If your system uses floppies, decide ahead of time how you will file and store material and then stick to that system. For example, if you decide to file by subject, use a separate disk for each. At the end of the semester you can always combine subjects on a single disk to save disk storage.

Hint: When roommates or friends share a computer, color code disks so that each of you can find his or her own disk easily.

If you work on a hard disk, set up this disk carefully. Read your manual for advice. If you follow instructions, you'll get more out of your investment. For example, the computer can work more efficiently when you set up many smaller files rather than lumping lots of material into fewer larger files. Because hard disks are expensive, it makes sense to make the most out of them.

Older Students, Other Problems 10

Up until now we've addressed this book to young (17- through 22-year-old) college students and to the personal, academic, economic, and social demands on their time. Today, however, mature reentry students—both men and women—make up a large percentage of the collegiate population. If you are a 30-, 40-, or 50-year-old college student with a family, you know that you face other kinds of pressures.

Socially, you may not be worried about dating. Instead, you worry about babysitters. Academically, you feel this is your opportunity to show what you can do, so those As and Bs become a measure of your self-worth. Personally, although you have another life outside of the campus, you still want to fit in. And economically, while your lab partner ponders how best to approach Mommy and Daddy for some more money, in fact you are Mommy or Daddy. So, after class, while your partner writes pleading letters, you go home to sweat over the unpaid bills.

In many ways the mature student's lot is more difficult. Used to being in charge in a job or at home, reentry students are suddenly taking instead of giving orders. School becomes one more demanding component of an already busy life requiring dedication and, above all, time. Reentry students often admit that if they could have one wish granted, that wish would be more time in their days.

☐ SIMPLIFY AND DELEGATE TO SURVIVE

To win the battle against time, you must add two more time-saving skills to your arsenal. Reentering students must also learn how to *simplify* and to *delegate.* If you don't apply these two principles of time management, no matter how skillfully you plan, identify goals, set priorities, and estimate time demands, no matter how faithfully you practice the Time Slots system, you will never feel like you've caught up.

First, you must enlist your family's support in your efforts. Explain to everyone involved that there will be some changes in all your lives. You won't have the time to do all the things you used to do for and with them. Some of these changes may be major. If you've been your son's math tutor, spending hours after dinner with him to work out algebra problems, he'll have to seek help elsewhere now that you have your own homework. Other changes may be more subtle. Dinner may be 45 minutes later because of your school schedule. Your spouse and children may be forced to become more self-sufficient and to adapt to your schedule at times. Often your going back to school means new responsibilities for them.

If you make time to explain your plans and goals far enough in advance, you should be able to minimize negative reaction. (Unfortunately, not all families are supportive, and in these instances, effective time management is crucial for your survival.)

Simplifying

Once you have your family on your side, examine your family's habits. You will be amazed at what you can find to simplify.

Begin by scrutinizing how you use your time at home. Ask yourself what you can do to make effective changes in your routine.

☐ If you spend time doing dishes on weekends when you really need to be studying, the switch to paper plates and cups can give you extra valuable minutes in your day you can use for school.

☐ While you may have enjoyed cooking elaborate meals during the week, planning simpler recipes and serving occasional frozen dinners won't hurt anyone.

☐ As for entertaining, restaurants are your best timesaver. Taking others out to lunch or dinner instead of cooking for those wonderful small dinner parties you are known for may work better for you now. If you prefer having guests in, plan casual bring-your-favorite-dish picnics or Sunday night suppers for the crowd.

☐ If gardening is your pride and joy, you will hate to give it up entirely. Instead of using the full yard, maximizing your time might mean minimizing your garden. Plant a corner of the yard or discover the fun of gardening in pots.

☐ Simplify your buying habits. Although you pride yourself on sending unique cards and unusual presents for special occasions, now you probably won't have the hours to spend browsing through shops selecting gifts and cards individually. If you find a birthday card you like, buy a dozen. Purchase generic gifts in quantity—items like pens or gourmet foods—which work for almost anyone for almost any occasion. Become a catalogue shopper and shop by mail or use your home computer to shop during those extra odd minutes.

Simplifying often means doing the minimum rather than the optimum. Shortcuts are essential for your well-being. The key, here, is to identify those time-consuming routines and then reduce the time they take by simplifying them. This can be something as simple as only clearing a path instead of shoveling the snow off the entire sidewalk. Simplifying is just another way to "take small bites."

Delegating

As you analyze your home life, look for opportunities to delegate responsibilities. Like simplifying, delegating allows you to put time back into your life. This is one of the most difficult time-saving skills to master because the natural inclination is that "it's easier to do myself."

The Successful Delegator Identifies

What he or she *wants* to do.
What he or she *needs* to do.
What can be *done by others.*

What you may want to do is chuck everything and run off to a deserted island. However, what you may need to do is get an English paper written, the groceries bought, a birthday gift wrapped, the bathrooms cleaned, and your checkbook balanced. Not all your wants and needs are so clearly delineated, of course, but by identifying and separating them as best you can, you can put these wants and needs in perspective.

The key to delegating is deciding what can be done by others. In the above example, only you can write that English paper. And if you are single, the checkbook is also your responsibility. But the other items are open to negotiation. Depending upon the ages and willingness of your children, you can enlist their help. Send a teenager to the store. Let a small child wrap a birthday gift. Assign the cleaning of the bathroom on a rotating basis—a different person each week.

Successful delegating involves more than assigning jobs. Once you have identified jobs that others can do, you must do advance planning. For instance, unless you want to take your chances for the week's groceries, make a list before sending someone else to the store. Before a child can wrap a gift, have wrapping paper and tape on hand. And if you want the bathrooms to remain safe for human habitation, make sure cleansers are available.

You may also need to alter your expectations. It is possible that the grocery person will return without cereal. It is probable that your young child will wrap a lumpy gift. And it is likely that your bathrooms won't gleam with the same shine you can give them. Greater delegating usually means lesser expectations. Everybody gets better with practice.

☐ REACH FOR YOUR TIME SLOTS

Your weekly Time Slots is a valuable support tool. It's a visual reminder of all your time demands. When you see everything you are doing, you feel less guilty about fingerprints on the cabinets, drips on the mirrors, overgrown grass, and peeling housepaint.

☐ Make copies of your weekly planner and tape one to the refrigerator where everyone sees it. Your family can see which are your light and which your heavy days, when you have classes, appointments, etc. You might not be home, but at least they know why.

☐ Consider giving a copy to your babysitter, children's grandparent, day care center, etc., so that your schedule is known in case you must be reached. This Time Slots form can be an excellent timesaver during an emergency, especially for a single parent.

☐ Keep another weekly Time Slots for your family's schedule. Record everyone's fixed activities on it and post it. You won't be able to resolve every conflict, but at least you'll keep track of each other.

☐ Use another weekly Time Slots form for household chores. Post it in a convenient spot to minimize "nobody ever told me's." When filling in this form remember that everyone can do something to help.

Use a PAP form to schedule family projects. Divide these into smaller, timely bites. If the house needs painting, list the various steps needed to accomplish this project, along with the person (or people) responsible for each step. Include a deadline for each segment of the job.

☐ AND STILL MORE TIMESAVERS . . .

Do double (or even triple) time. Perfect the art of doing two things at once or even three or more if you can handle it. As you mow the lawn, memorize chemical charts. As you catch up on housework, listen to your taped notes. If you drive in a carpool, ask your child to quiz you for an exam. When you are in the college bookstore, buy collegiate gifts: sweatshirts, pens, mugs, etc. These make great gifts for your children, who will love to feel part of your school life. The more you perfect this art, the more inventive you will become and the more ways you'll find to do two or more things at once.

Never be without a text, notecards, and pencil. Train yourself to carry a book, notecards, and pencil with you. If you bike to and from campus, keep notecards and a spare pencil in your backpack. If you drive, keep these supplies in your car. Never walk out the door without a text you need to study. This way, instead of standing and fuming while waiting in a long line to change a class or reading a children's magazine in the pediatrician's waiting room, you can read and underline a chapter of text. Instead of shopping for those 45 minutes while your daughter takes her french horn lesson, you can study.

Enjoy lost time. Using your organizational skills you'll discover time you didn't know you had—so-called "lost time." This could be a "found" 35 minutes when you scheduled an appointment for an hour, and it took just 25 minutes. It could be an extra 15 minutes you discover you don't need to spend on an assignment. Or you might make all the lights and miss heavy traffic and arrive home 10 minutes earlier than usual. Make a commitment to yourself to put this time to good use. Of course, you can use a half hour to read over notes, but you might also sit down for a chat with your child, fix that lamp that flickers, or just relax. Don't be afraid to simply enjoy this extra time.

Lost time can provide needed breathers in busy schedules, but you should also schedule some time just for you, alone. This isn't a selfish gesture. You need time to do nothing, to read a novel, to work a puzzle, to watch television or nap. Think of these as refueling stops in your hectic schedule. Without them, you won't be able to run.

Take time out. Save some time just for you and your spouse or friend. You may both experience strong emotions as each of you adjusts to a life which the other isn't always part of. You may feel guilty and jealous; your spouse or friend may feel beleaguered or lonely. Making time just for each other can smooth this rough adjustment.

Save some time for each child as well. The key here is to give each child individual attention. You might plan to take one shopping and out to dinner, leaving the other home with your spouse. Dinner can be a hotdog at the shopping mall. The food is less important than the company. Treat each child to a ballgame, alone with you. Or turn a chore into a game for the two of you, racing to see who can clean the bookshelves faster or rake the yard better. Be cognizant of the changes you are asking your children to make and be considerate of them. Money may be short just now, but your time and attention is the best gift you can give at any time.

Don't believe for a minute that you can save time for yourself, your spouse, and your children every day and still meet your academic and other commitments. However, by organizing and managing your time, you can work in some time for everyone—eventually.

How to Get the Most Out of Even a Few Minutes

11

Using the Time Slots forms will give you more time in your life. As you plan your weeks and days more effectively and work more efficiently, you will find that you discover extra, free minutes and hours. You may finish an assignment faster than you anticipated. Or, thanks to your efficient planning, complete a meeting faster than you expected. There are all kinds of ways that extra time appears in your life once you get organized.

The problem is that often we feel that 5 or even 45 minutes is not enough time to get started, let alone really do something. This isn't so! As you learn the Time Slots system, you'll come up with all kinds of ideas of your own for these small blocks of time. But for now, here's a quick time plan showing what you can do in just 5, 15, 30, or 45 minutes.

Where can you uncover an extra 5 minutes? That's easy. You can get through dinner quicker than usual (nobody liked the menu, so there wasn't a line), finish studying 5 minutes ahead of time, finish jogging in a faster-than-usual time, or catch the bus home without any waiting. So what can you do with this time? Not much, you say? Think again.

The Five-Minute Fanatic Can . . .

Set up a place to study for the day.

Do a relaxation exercise to calm the mind before studying for an exam.

Organize class notes in preparation for studying.

Put in a load of laundry (but not permanent press unless you will also be there to take it out when it's done!).

Enjoy some stretching exercises to improve alertness.

Suppose you planned to call home—saving 15 minutes to catch up on everyone's doings—and nobody answered. Or suppose a meeting you promised to attend is called off, or you made every green light and arrived home early, or you had planned to go to the drugstore but discovered you HAD shampoo. What would you do with these new 15 minutes? Relax? Or regroup?

The Fifteen-Minute Organizer Can . . .

Review class notes.
Plan the next day's activity schedule.
Make an appointment with a professor either before or after class.
Balance a stubborn checkbook and find an error.
Hand wash some clothes.
Study for a quiz.
Phone home to ask for cash to cover the error.
Outline a term paper assignment.
Do 15 minutes of aerobics or calisthenics.
Write a letter that's owed.
Put an ad in the campus newspaper advertising a business service, i.e., typing, delivering pizzas, dog walking, etc. Put class notes on tape (a favorite trick of successful graduate students since this enables you to flesh out your notes and remember them more completely).

Have you ever had an appointment with a professor only to have the office call to cancel it? Or gone to the library and found that the book you need isn't available? Or attended a meeting which adjourned a half hour early? Or written a paper in barely 2 hours which you had estimated would take 2½ hours? Or planned to go to the post office only to find it's Columbus Day, and it is closed?

Given an entire half hour, you could sleep or talk or shop, but . . .

The Down and Dirty Thirty-Minute Master Can . . .

Go to the bank if it's near.
Get some information on a scholarship.
Study the help-wanted ads looking for a part-time job.
Pick up supplies at the bookstore.
Read a short assignment (five to seven pages).

Outline a course project (provided it's been thought out in advance!).

Meet with an advisor.

Meet with another professor.

Exercise.

Study with someone else by outlining the areas a test may cover.

At times you may even find 45 minutes you didn't plan for. A class is cancelled or a doctor's appointment runs on time. Your roommate bought groceries so you don't have to shop, or if you commute, you make all your connections. If you usually coach junior high soccer that day, practice is rained out. Less organized people might just go for coffee, but . . .

The Forty-Five Minute Mogul Can . . .

Complete a short assignment in the library.

Read ten–fifteen pages (average) in an average text.

Outline a chapter of a text.

Type a three–six page paper.

Pick up concert tickets on campus.

Interview for a part-time job.

Nap (getting refreshed before studying again, taking care not to oversleep!).

Do a computer search for a term paper.

Sharpen typing skills.

☐ DON'T FORGET DOUBLETIME

Don't believe it when people say you can't do two things at once! You just have to be selective as to which two things. You can . . .

Exercise while listening to taped class notes.

Listen to the news while you get dressed.

Read an assignment while waiting for an appointment.

Review class notes while standing in line (college means *lots* of lines).

Complete assignments while waiting for the laundry to get finished.

Recite mathematical formulas or history dates or practice a foreign language—aloud—while cleaning.

☐ FOUR WAYS FOR FRESHMEN TO BEAT THE MAZE

For freshmen who have never been on campus before, here are some additional practical pointers to save you time and frustration. Since each of these helps you anticipate situations, you can avoid time crunches and potential crises.

1. *Obtain the information available from each department.* Every department has all kinds of facts on classes, teachers, course load, and special requirements. All you have to do is ask at the department office, in advance, when you consider taking a course within that department. Amazingly, few students use this valuable, ever-ready resource.

2. *Make time to get to know your advisor.* It's up to you to make an impression. Once you do, your advisor can provide excellent advice and support. Telephone or stop in first to set up an appointment. Come to that appointment prepared with some questions about specific courses, teachers, departments, or activities. Act professional.

3. *Learn what it takes to get into the various classes that interest you.* The word to watch for is "prerequisite." Chances are, you can't take French 3 unless you've taken French 1 and 2. That one's easy. Other course requirements are less obvious. Read the fine print in the catalogue; ask upperclassmen, your advisor, or the instructor about prerequisites and what, if any, exceptions are made before you stand in line all those hours to sign up for classes.

4. *Be a budget miser—as well as a timesaver.* Often students spend more time worrying about money than courses. Money is a major concern for almost any college student. Save yourself hours of worry and frustration by finding out where you can get price breaks on books, groceries, furniture, appliances, etc.

College towns are the original flea markets. "Used" students are your best line to the "used" world. Ask and you shall receive, at half price or even less), and in much less time than you would have thought possible.

Other Ways to Use the Time Slots Forms

12

Once you get your immediate life in order—your course work and your weekly and daily schedules—you may want to use the Time Slots forms in other ways. Both the CRP and the PAP can go to work for you outside of class.

☐ THE PAP AS A FINANCIAL PLANNER

Use this Time Slots form for financial planning. This is different from setting up an annual or monthly budget. Financial planning requires that you identify a strategy to get your finances in shape. You must assess your situation, set objectives, and devise the method to meet these objectives. Your PAP can be an invaluable aid. It lets you see the big picture, and your budget becomes your tool to help you implement your strategy.

Begin by listing your present financial needs on a piece of scrap paper. For example, tuition and books may be paid for, yet you may be responsible for:

Fraternity/sorority dues
Transportation: car payments, bus fares, subway fees
Clothes
Haircuts, etc.
Spending money
Gifts
Medical and dental fees

Ask yourself what amount you need to cover these expenses and then add a fudge factor to cover splurges, unexpected crises, and happy surprises.

What expenses do you have coming up in the next few months? What will they add to your overall expenses? Consider birthday gifts, Christmas, getting your teeth cleaned—in short, anything that you know will happen that will require dipping into your wallet.

Now write a second list which takes stock of your income. If the figure is dismal, think about ways you can increase that amount. How much can you earn tutoring? Do you plan to get a job in a restaurant? Can you put in some hours as a library assistant? Multiply the hours you work (or plan to work) times the salary, and then subtract withholding fees, so that you know what amount is your take-home pay.

Quick figuring gives you a rough idea of what it costs to support you in the academic and social style you want to enjoy.

Having done the preliminary research, reach for your PAP and your pencil.

Putting the PAP to Work

To begin your financial planning, take a PAP form and fill out the top. Under *Project Title,* write "Financial Needs." (As you think about your checking account, with its negative balance, you may smile at the understatement.) You decide that six months is a realistic time frame for putting your new financial planning into effect and write "1-1-91 to 6-1-91" under the project due date. This is Winter/Spring '91.

Under the project outline column, you list your financial needs as you see them. You take care not to bog yourself down in detailed planning. You'll do that later. For now you concentrate only on your current needs. In the financial needs column, you list:

Bodywork on car—$600
Pay back loan to Uncle Jim—$150
Apartment fund—$1,000 (so can move out of dorm!)
Survival—clear $100 a month (for 6 months) after expenses so not living hand to mouth

Next you set your financial priorities. You decide which item on the list to attack first. At first glance, they all seem critical. But as you rethink them, priorities emerge.

Survival, you know, is crucial. Somehow you've got to come up with $100 a month. If you don't, you can cancel the rest of the list. So survival is Number 1. Fixing your car is your second priority. The passenger door doesn't close properly, and it's getting cold. Paying back that loan deserves attention next, and, finally, you want to put away money so you can eventually move into an apartment. These are 3 and 4.

When you add up the dollars, you gulp. The grand total is $2,350.

Now you must set realistic deadlines to accomplish each financial goal. Number 1 has to happen immediately! Somehow you must assure a steady income. As for the body work, you decide to carry a blanket in the car until Spring. You can't get to that until March. Finally, you target June as the month to have the loan paid and the apartment fund completed. You write each of these dates under the *Due Date* column.

The analysis column is your place to work out on paper how you are going to pay for each financial priority. You go back to your income list and reread it, considering all sources of income and analyzing your resources.

You can come up with that $100 a month if you cut way back on your spending. Good-bye, tapes and concert tickets. Hello, generic foods. As you work through each of your priorities, you write down a plan of action under the *Analysis* column next to each need. Your creative juices flow. You can sell your old skis, tutor, borrow some money from your apartment fund, and work overtime. And there's always birthday money. You can also use this column to keep track of the money you earn. For example, when you sell the skis, you write "$75" next to that entry. You will need to add and delete information from the PAP. Windfalls occur. You could win a lottery, or your roommate could pay back that loan you wrote off long ago. Unexpected expenses can also befall you. As changes occur in your financial status, revise your analysis, change your priorities, and reassess deadlines.

When you arrive at your goal, save your PAP. You will be doubly rewarded because not only have you achieved what you set out to do, but you have a detailed outline of how you did it. You may find that you will be able to use this same strategy again to effect a similar success. Build on your winnings.

☐ THE CRP AS AN ACTIVITY PLANNER

When you say "yes" to club or committee work, reach for the CRP. Not only will it help you keep track of your progress, it will also help you determine a timeline, that is, give you a way to set your objectives and key them to your calendar.

Let's say that a campus political group has approached you to run a fundraising activity. You decide to run a goods and services auction. Checking the campus calendar, you select April 20th as your date.

Reach for the CRP (in this case your "club requirement planner"). Under the heading *Course* write "Campus Fundraiser—Goods & Services Auction."

Then you think through the major steps to run such an auction.

Under the *Course Requirement* column, you write these steps:

Contact other clubs, dorms, etc., to get G&S
Arrange for auctioneer
Find location—make physical arrangements
Publicity
Program
Entertainment?

Filling in the *Date Due* column is easy. You write the date of the auction—4/20—under each *Date Due* box.

Reading through the various parts of the project, you decide that finding a location is first priority; contacting clubs, etc., for goods and services your second; arranging for an auctioneer the next step, followed by getting publicity rolling. You save the program and possible entertainment for the final two steps. You number each item according to its sequence in the *Order to be Done* column.

Remembering that planning begins long-range and moves to short-range, you work backwards from the auction date to estimate time needs. As you consider each segment of the project and estimate the time required to accomplish each, you note your estimate under total time estimate.

You see that you have two and a half months to get everything done. Since you have lots of ideas about the location and need to compare costs and availability of each, you give yourself six weeks to get this lined up and write "six weeks" under the *Total Time Estimate* column. Attracting the G&S is the most important part of the fundraiser, so you target six weeks for that as well. You can arrange for an auctioneer in a week. As your assistant chairperson is handling publicity, you'll leave that up to her, but you give yourself a month to book entertainment. Finally, you figure the program can be done in a week, even taking into account last minute changes.

Working back from your time estimates, you assign starting dates for each and note those dates under *Date Start.*

As you assign jobs to various people, you give a copy of this plan to each person involved. Every other week, when you hold a committee meeting, you go over the timeline to see if it is still realistic and make necessary adjustments.

You also ask each person who is assigned to a particular job to fill in the actual date he or she began working on a particular segment of the project if it differs from the date you wrote in. This simple request can save misunderstandings. Nobody can say, "You didn't tell me to" or "I didn't know." And you can tell quickly who needs to be spurred on, who is doing a great job, and what potential problems loom ahead.

As you and your committee work through the project, everyone involved jots down the date each step is completed under the *Date Completed* column. As you review the progress of the project, you see how easy it is to underestimate time. For example, although you had thought finding a location would be easy, it wasn't until the end of March that the location was finalized. You planned to spend six weeks lining up auction items, and this actually took nine weeks. But the biggest surprise was the auctioneer. Although one of your friends assured you he had "connections," he didn't come through. You had to scramble for a month to come up with an auctioneer.

□ THE CRP AS A GOAL PLANNER

The CRP also works well as a goal planner. Because it prompts you to work on a deadline, it can help you end up with a solid plan for action instead of a wish list.

In September, Jamie decided to make 1990–91 her year. She got out her CRP and wrote "1990–91 Goals" at the top. Then she listed all she hoped to accomplish. She wanted to get a B in history by the end of the second semester. She needed to line up a summer job. She wanted to organize her course work. Since she never felt she expressed herself as forcefully as she could, she decided to take a public speaking course during the year. And she vowed to get into shape. Last, she added that she wanted to get into a campus musical organization because this is where she thought she'd meet people with similar interests.

As she read over her goals, she decided that each was realistic. Careful not to overload herself, she decided to focus on one of her two main priorities—getting her work organized and getting a B in history second semester—each semester. That way she could work on one main goal and two minor ones—certainly a manageable load.

She gave each goal a numbered priority, writing the appropriate number under the *Order to be Done* column. Getting organized was number 1 for this semester. Unless she did that, she couldn't do anything else. She would focus on her history grade, her second most important goal, next semester. Taking a public speaking course, she admitted, was also important to her. She made that number 3. And she assigned the campus organization, exercise, and getting a summer job 4, 5, and 6. The job was important, but she felt she had plenty of time to find one.

Working long-range to short-range, under the *Date Due* column Jamie wrote the date by which each goal should be accomplished. She targeted October 1 for getting organized. She wanted that B by the end of second semester, May 30. She decided to save her public speaking course for second semester as well. She needed to complete it by May 30. She wanted to get into an active on-campus musical group by November 1. Rather than put off an exercise program any longer, she gave herself until September 30 to be involved in a physical fitness program. Last, she planned to line up a summer job by April 30.

With her target dates set, she estimated the time needed to accomplish each goal and recorded this under *Total Time Estimate.* She wanted to get organized within three weeks after classes started. The B average would take the entire second semester, or four and a half months. She estimated her public speaking course would also take an entire semester, but felt she could join an on-campus group within a month after she got organized and knew for sure how much time she could devote to such an activity. She gave herself a month to get going on exercise. And she figured it would take her four and a half months to find a job.

Next Jamie picked her target dates to begin working on achieving each goal. As she selected these dates, she wrote them under the *Date Start* column. Organization would have to start the first day of classes, September 10. She would concentrate on history at the beginning of second semester, January 10. She'd start public speaking January 10 and begin investigating campus musical organizations October 1. She would start looking for an exercise program now, before classes begin. As for the summer job, she would start looking during Christmas vacation.

As she worked on each goal, Jamie wrote down victory dates under the *Date Completed* column. Before she went out to celebrate each achievement, she reread her CRP goal planner. Some of her estimates, she learned, were way off. For instance, while she thought getting organized would take three weeks, it took five. She had also underestimated how long it would take to find a summer job. Instead of four and a half months, it took her five and a half months. On the other hand, she overestimated the amount of time to find and join the campus choir. And she realized that by the first of May, thanks to being organized, she had actually assured at least a B+ in history.

As you continue using your Time Slots, no doubt you will think of other ways these planning tools can help you organize the many demands in your life. Be creative and have a good time.

Visualizing Time 13

Accelerating Time

Getting through college successfully has a lot to do with attitude. And attitudes can be tricky.

Consider, for instance, the current attitude about time. You don't have to be a genius to see we live in a speed-driven culture, a rapidly accelerating world in which people are rewarded for doing more things faster. Acceleration or "self-push," as it is often described, can overwhelm us because the more we accelerate, the more we find to do and the more difficult it becomes to keep up with, let alone step off, the merry-go-round. We may also become addicted to this behavior, which complicates our lives even more. Living at a breakneck pace is like living on the edge of danger. It's exciting but risky. No matter how busy we are and how much we accomplish, once we become addicted to acceleration, we never feel we're doing enough. Acceleration then is not only a self-fullfilling prophecy, it can become a self-defeating habit.

Acceleration feels like this. 7:30 A.M. The alarm rings. You spring out of bed. Late. You meant to set the clock for 6:00 A.M. You need to study. You're already behind!

You hit the shower. Jump into your clothes. Gulp down some coffee and a danish. Eat while scanning your sociology text. Jog to class, reviewing the day. Cycling club tonight. Speak to French conversation partner. Study for economics quiz. Finish article for the literary magazine. Inquire about staff positions for next year. Study. Tennis date. Oops. Job interview tomorrow. Check wardrobe today.

You reach class. Your head is swimming. You take a deep breath. Concentrate on the test. Rush to the next class. The prof pops a quiz. On to Appointments. Meetings. Lab. Check your watch. Don't be late. More to do. Don't stop.

Midnight. You're edgy and fatigued. Red eyed, you look up

from your textbook. You know you're organized. You've accomplished nearly everything you intended to do. Yet, despite your accomplishments, you don't feel satisfied. You spend so much time trying to keep up with time that you are a slave to the clock.

If the pace of these paragraphs describe your life, you may be caught up in accelerating time. You aren't alone. Americans are consumed by time. Frenetic is our national state. More than any other people, we cram our calendars with activities, appointments and events. We feel compelled to fill up every waking moment. We sleep less, play less, and work more. We run full tilt and then wonder why we are exhausted and uptight.

If you're not sure if you fit the profile, answer these questions.

Do you often feel emotionally out of breath, as if you are running and can't keep up?

Do you feel guilty when, after accomplishing your main objectives, you take time out to relax?

Do you find that you are lost without a wristwatch and constantly check the clock?

Do you pride yourself on your packed schedule?

Do you constantly feel there's more you must do?

If you answered yes to most of these questions, you need extra support to relieve the pressures of accelerating time. The Time Slots program provides a basic approach for organizing your day, week, and month. But it doesn't address the issue of acceleration. In this speed-driven world, it's important that you know how to get back in touch with yourself so you can quiet your mind, stop focusing on the clock, and decelerate.

There are many ways to accomplish this. One avenue is mental imagery. This approach works well because your mind is your most powerful organizational tool. By focusing your mind, you can change the way you perceive stressful situations and, therefore, make better use of your time.

Why Mental Imagery?

Like physical exercise, visualization or mental imagery can have a profoundly relaxing effect. When practiced regularly, it allows you to slow down from the inside while still keeping pace with your busy college life.

Visualization isn't mystical or magical. Although the term

implies "seeing" something, you *can* visualize without sound or pictures. Everyone visualizes differently. Some people actually "see" images. It's as if they are equipped with mental VCRs they can turn on at will. Others receive audio signals which help them talk their way through situations. And still other people experience a strong emotional response as they think about a certain problem or upcoming meeting. Whatever works for you is right. Don't analyze the process. Just let it happen.

There are two forms of visual imagery—the receptive and the active mode. In the receptive state, you relax and allow impressions or "pictures" to come freely to the surface of your conscious thought. You don't intentionally paint a scene. You think about a situation and the image or conversation or feeling occurs.

In the active mode, you create what you wish to see or imagine. You deliberately select details or hear conversations to help set the stage. Because you control what you want to "see," active visualization is easiest to learn and practice.

The following exercises and techniques are all in the active mode.

The purpose of these visualizations is to provide you with another set of tools to help you get through time-pressured situations. The four areas that are targeted in the following visualizations are the most frequent problem areas for college students. Because each produces stress, each situation prevents you from using time to your best advantage. Just as the Time Slots forms are physical time management aids, these visualizations are mental tools. Combining the Time Slots system with a mental imagery program enables you to be more relaxed about time and more efficient in using it. You'll find, as you practice these visualizations, you will accomplish more and feel better about yourself.

These four exercises provide a basic visualization program. As you practice them, you may wish to learn more about the power of visualization. Shakti Gawain's *Creative Visualization* (Bantam, 1982) is an excellent resource.

4 VISUALIZATIONS FOR TIME-PRESSURED STUDENTS

You'll need 15 minutes of privacy to practice each of these exercises. Find a place where you are comfortable and won't be interrupted by friends or the telephone. If you use your room, post a "Do Not Interrupt" sign on the door and let people know you mean it. If your popularity suffers, take solace that your grades will improve!

Always begin by settling into a comfortable position in which you can take deep breaths regularly and easily. Don't slouch. Sit straight in a chair with both feet touching the floor. This position invites a positive energy flow.

Begin each visualization with relaxation. For any visualization to be effective, you must be completely relaxed. If you don't have a favorite relaxation technique, try circular breathing. It's easy and it works.

Circular Breathing Relaxation

With your eyes gently closed, take a deep, slow breath. Slowly let that breath out. Immediately take another deep, slow breath. Let that breath escape slowly. See a circle forming from your inhale to your exhale. Inhale again with a deep, slow breath. Continue circular breathing until you feel totally relaxed and at peace. This usually takes about three to five minutes.

Once you are completely relaxed, you are ready to practice visualization.

Visualization Exercise One

Handling Overload: *Blow It Off*

Sometimes, no matter how hard you try to organize yourself, you feel overloaded and overwhelmed. Once these feelings begin to build, pressure mounts. This creates a cycle that is difficult to break.

What can you do?

Try this visualization. It is great for stressful moments.

Create a visual image of a time when you felt overwhelmed as a result of your schedule. Maybe you had two tests in one week plus your parttime job, *and* you promised your roommate to type a paper for him. Recall the physical sensations you experienced as you went into overload. Was your neck tight? Shoulders tense? Jaw ache? Did your head pound?

Recall your emotional response. Were you angry? Frustrated? Anxious? Miserable?

For a few moments, relive this stressful time.

Now take a deep breath and as you exhale, see and feel those overwhelming sensations floating away.

Continue to inhale and exhale slowly until you have blown away all those unhappy and unhealthy feelings. Calm and relaxed, you can easily identify what caused your stress in that situation.

Affirmation: Complete this exercise with this affirmation. "Organizing my time comes easily to me."

Affirmations are a simple way of sealing your intentions. By stating your situation in a positive way, you "make firm" your resolve.

Whenever you slip into overload, try this visualization technique. First, relax with deep breathing. Then procede to the visualization exercise, recalling a tense time and then "blowing away" every negative sensation. Always finish the exercise with the affirmation.

Visualization Exercise Two

Counter-Productive Attitudes: *Rehearse It First*

Counterproductive time habits are difficult to break. Take procrastination. Chances are you vow *not* to procrastinate. You start out with the best intentions. You announce to everyone that this time you are going to start early and finish early. But somehow you sabotage yourself. Suddenly you have a paper due in a week, and you haven't even started. Or, the semester ends, and your independent assignments aren't complete.

What can you do? Use this visualization whenever you sense trouble as a result of untimely habits. This particular exercise is designed to handle procrastination since it is the most common time problem for college students. But once you learn this technique, you can adapt it to create visualizations for any other problem area. The key is to intentionally "rehearse" a *constructive* habit so that it becomes natural for you, rather than repeat that old, counterproductive method.

Begin with relaxation. Once you are calm and feel peaceful, imagine this scenario.

You have been assigned a project to complete for linguistics class. It's a required course that you aren't excited about, but you must take it to graduate. Your usual way of completing projects and term papers is waiting until the week before the due date to begin work. This time you decide to try a new approach to create some excitement about this class.

Since you have six weeks to complete it, you decide to work on this project week by week. In week one you create an outline and start researching in the library. You set deadlines of what needs to be done by the end of each week.

As you imagine yourself researching, you start getting excited about the information you find. Because you have time to work on this, you are happy and relaxed.

Move to the final week. "See" yourself doing the editing and typing. Two days before the due date, see yourself having completed the project. You feel calm, happy, and proud about the good job you have done.

Watch yourself turn in the project. You are smiling and laughing to yourself about how you put it together with time to spare. Leave class and reward yourself with an afternoon of total relaxation.

Finally, picture yourself receiving an A for this project. It's clear that your old way of working made projects more difficult. This new way is easier and much more fun.

Affirmation: Complete the visualization with this affirmation. "I can easily change my attitudes about time."

Use this mental exercise whenever you feel you are slipping into an uncomfortable and inefficient habit. Each time you run through this scenario, it will become more natural for you to paint the image you want. Do not skip any steps. Walk yourself through the situation in as much detail as possible. The more real you make it, the more effective this visualization becomes.

Visualization Exercise Three

Maintaining Your Balance: *Rise Above It*

It's not easy to juggle the big four demands of college: academics, money, social life, and personal responsibilities. Sometimes, pushed and pulled by demands on your time, you may feel like you are out of balance.

When this occurs, chances are, you need help. Balance is an emotional as well as physical state. Whenever we are excessively pressured by time, we can lose our emotional equilibrium.

Each of us has a natural state of balance which is as instinctive as breathing, as innate as our pulse rates. This state of balance is closely tuned to our perception of time. We feel balanced when our actions and thoughts are aligned with our natural rhythms and pace. Conversely, we can move out of balance when we ignore our own time cues and concentrate too much on meeting others' schedules and expectations.

Try this exercise whenever you feel that you are losing your sense of balance because of all the commitments on your time. Better yet, practice this exercise daily, even if you don't think you need it. Balance is such a delicate state that even a slight correction can make you feel lots better.

Begin with deep circular breathing. Once you establish an easy rhythm and feel at ease, visualize this scene.

With your eyes closed, imagine yourself floating on a cloud high above the earth. Concentrate on how it feels to drift along on this soft surface rocked by gentle breezes. Feel the cloud gently supporting your limbs and body much as water buoys you up as you float on your back. Feel your body shift as the cloud moves up and down, back and forth, to sense your balance. Indulge yourself in the sensation of weightlessness. Hold that picture and those feelings in your mind. Release them. Bring the scene up again. Let it go. See it once more. Release it.

Completely relaxed, recall a day or moment when you felt terrific about yourself. Maybe you received an A on an important test or made the last payment on your car. Whatever the image, relive the joy and satisfaction of that time. Remember how great you felt, how everything just fell into place. Savor that sense of being at ease and at peace.

Enjoy this moment. See it in as much detail as you can. Remember what you were wearing and where you were standing. Replay conversations. Feel the sunlight or cool breeze on your skin.

Now imagine feeling like this all the time. Seeing yourself in this state lets you consciously align your inner and outer environments. You intentionally create a state of equilibrium. Hold that image. Now let it fade.

Affirmation: Complete this visualization with this statement. "Time is my friend. I work and live at my own pace."

As you practice this visualization, you'll notice some changes occur. Your breathing may become more relaxed. You may lose that desparate sense of "rushing." Physical tensions may lessen. Such physical signs tell you that you are getting back in balance.

Be aware, however, that the goal of this exercise is not simply to slow down. Rather, it is to become consciously tuned to your own natural rhythms and pace. The more you recognize your own state of balance, the easier it is for you to create this condition deliberately.

One word of caution. Everyone has his or her own natural rhythms. Your pace may not be comfortable for your roommate or best friend. As each of you comes to terms with your own rhythms, you'll see that pace does make a difference in relationships. Happily, however, as you become more tuned to your own state of balance, you'll also become more sensitive to others' rhythms. Such knowledge won't change ingrained habits, but it will help you better understand your roommate and friends.

Quick Course Correction

Both happy surprises and unexpected glitches can throw you off balance. To get back on center fast, try this quick course correction.

Visualize a teeter totter. See it perfectly balanced. In this position, you feel most at ease. Allow the board to move up and down a bit. Then watch as it settles into a level position. Take a deep breath in. Exhale slowly. Repeat. Then say aloud the affirmation: "Time is my friend. I work and live at my own pace."

Check your state of balance by bringing the teeter totter

image to mind. If one side is up and other end is down, you are out of sync with your natural pace. Breathe in and out easily. Gently allow the teeter totter to settle in a level position. As you watch it, feel yourself regain your sense of equilibrium.

Visualization Exercise Four

Preparing for Projects and Tests: *Positive Energy*

Big tests and major projects can be anxiety producing. Even well-prepared students experience some stress before an important exam. Such excess stress is a time problem because it can be counterproductive. Instead of focusing on the job at hand, you focus on your fear.

This exercise is designed to help change that focus so you deal directly with the exam or project. By practicing this visualization, you teach yourself to create positive experiences out of challenging situations.

Begin with deep, rhythmical, circular breathing. Once you are completely relaxed and at ease, picture this.

See that test or project as a bright star. Notice the glowing colors it emits.

Place it in the night sky. See this star as a source of positive energy. This energy represents the knowledge you have to succeed on that test or project.

Allow it to explode. As the star bursts into streaks and flashes of light, feel your anxiety about the test or project dissolve with the star.

Feel the force of that exploded star as positive energy. Experience that flow of energy throughout your mind and body.

Continue to breathe deeply and enjoy this energized sensation.

Affirmation: Complete this visualization with this affirmation. "I see this test/project as a positive experience at which I will succeed."

Use this exercise when you feel yourself tensing up over a major project or exam. You can do this visualization the night before an exam or even just before you begin to take the test. This visualization transforms negative anxiety into positive energy.

☐ GETTING UNSTUCK

These four exercises comprise a basic visual imagery package. The techniques sound easy, and they are—as long as they work. But sometimes, despite your best intentions, you can get stuck. No matter how hard you try to visualize, your mental VCR won't click on. Your mind is blocked. What do you do?

Blocks are caused by repressed emotions such as fear, guilt, resentment, or anger. Any one of these can cause you to shut down. When this occurs, you need a new approach to work past the block.

First of all, be patient. Everyone blocks at some time or other. Second of all, be curious. When you run into a blank wall, be honest about the problem that's behind that wall. Are you afraid to succeed? Most of all, relax. Be kind to yourself. Take a break. Do something completely different. Then come back and try again. Generally, if you are patient, the block will disappear.

☐ ARE YOU HAVING FUN YET?

Using the Time Slots forms and practicing these four visualizations will help you feel more in control of yourself and your time. But there's one more factor for you to consider when planning your days and nights. That factor is *FUN.* If you aren't having any fun yet, you aren't making the best use of your time and talents.

What is fun? Fun can be the sense of enjoyment when you are doing something and lose yourself in the task. It can be a sense of accomplishment when you are finished with a difficult project. And it can be a feeling, when you look back on a project, that you are glad you did it. Fun can be as simple as a private moment sitting by the lake or as wild as a Friday night party. It can be as mild as a compliment from a professor or as intense as romance.

Whenever you think about taking on a responsibility—whether it's a committee chairmanship or signing up for a new course—let fun be your guide. Ask yourself if this task or course will be fun to do.

If something sounds like fun for you to do, you can be sure it suits your balance and rhythms. As a result, it won't add extra stress and pressure. If the element of fun isn't present, try to avoid that course or responsibility and find one that will be fun to do.

That's not to say that you won't get frustrated or tired or angry as you get into this course or work through the committee. Fun is an indication of your feelings as you consider a project. It's not a guarantee that your feelings won't change as you get into the nitty-gritty. Still, feeling positive, excited, or turned on about a job or subject when you begin it, greatly increases your chances for success. And in college, you need all the success you can get!

The Last Word

Even the most efficient and effective writers need a last word.

We've given you four tools—the four Time Slots forms—which can make your life easier and help you succeed in school. We hope you will use them.

We've talked about four time demands—academic, social, personal, and economic—and how you can use time management tools and techniques to relieve the pressures brought on by those demands. We hope, after you begin using these tools, you will find you do have less pressure and more time.

We now leave you with four final points:

1. *Time management works.* The system we've described—planning, identifying goals, estimating time demands, and setting priorities—works. If you practice these principles, they will work for you. The more you use them, the more natural they will become.
2. *The tools are essential.* Nothing works by itself. You need to spend time to save time. Reading this book is a great first step. But reading it once won't do it. You may need to reread sections. As you use this method, you may devise your own techniques for estimating time demands. That's fine as long as you remember to estimate. You'll definitely need to use the Time Slots.
3. *Time management will help you stay on track.* Don't panic if you fall off course. Everybody does except obsessive/compulsive personalities, and they don't have any fun. The beauty of the system is that since you know what you have to do, even if you don't do it all, you can always get started again.
4. *Time management skills and techniques are good for life.* Learning how to organize your time gives you an edge on balancing your life. Although this book and these tools are designed for college students, the forms, skills, and visualizations will grow with you through school and life.

You are living in a time of incredible change. Change is constant and fast. As this decade unfolds, you will need more than traditional time management techniques to feel comfortable in this accelerating age. Mental imagery combined with the Time Slots system provides you with the support you need not only to survive, but to thrive.

Happily, you only have to learn all of this once. Time management is a lot like riding a bicycle. Once you learn how to do it, you never forget.

Good luck!

Order Information

To order additional forms, contact: Time Systems, Inc. 5353 North 16th Street, Suite 400, Phoenix, AZ 85016-9864.

About the authors

DIANA SCHARF-HUNT, PH.D., is an educator, time management expert, and businesswoman. Presenting personal productivity seminars to young adults inspired her to develop the Time Slots system for students. A runner, skier, and horsewoman, Dr. Hunt finds time for it all by practicing what she teaches.

PAM HAIT, a graduate of Northwestern University's Medill School of Journalism, is a freelance writer whose work appears in many national magazines. She still is late for appointments, but now knows why.

Also by Diana Scharf-Hunt and Pam Hait: *The Tao of Time* (Holt, 1990).

COURSE REQUIREMENT PLANNER

COURSE:

ORDER TO BE DONE	COURSE REQUIREMNET	DUE DATE	TOTAL TIME EST.	DATE START	DATE COMPLETE

COURSE REQUIREMENT PLANNER

COURSE:

ORDER TO BE DONE	COURSE REQUIREMNET	DUE DATE	TOTAL TIME EST.	DATE START	DATE COMPLETE

PROJECT ASSIGNMENT PLANNER

COURSE:____

PROJECT TITLE:__________________________________

PROJECT DUE DATE:______________________________

SEMESTER/QUARTER:______________________________

Part	Project/Term Paper Outline	Analysis	Due Date

Part	Project/Term Paper Outline	Analysis	Due Date

WEEKLY PLANNER

MONTH ______________ WEEK OF ______________

	AM	PM
SUN		
MON		
TUE		
WED		
THUR		
FRI		
SAT		

WEEKLY PLANNER

MONTH ______________ WEEK OF ______________

	AM	PM
SUN		
MON		
TUE		
WED		
THUR		
FRI		
SAT		

DAILY PLANNER

Activties for: Sun Mon Tues Wed Thur Fri Sat
(CIRCLE ONE)

Time	Record or Schedule	B	A	Events
6				
7				
8				
9				
10				
11				
12				
1				
2				
3				
4				
5				
6				
7				
8				
9				
10				

DAILY PLANNER

Activties for: Sun Mon Tues Wed Thur Fri Sat
(CIRCLE ONE)

Time	Record or Schedule	B	A	Events
6				
7				
8				
9				
10				
11				
12				
1				
2				
3				
4				
5				
6				
7				
8				
9				
10